The Hard Question of Art

Contents

The Hard Question of Art

Cognitive Futures

Metahaven

VERSO
London • New York

First published by Verso 2026

The manufacturer's authorized representative in the EU
for product safety (GPSR) is LOGOS EUROPE,
9 rue Nicolas Poussin, 17000, La Rochelle, France
contact@logoseurope.eu

1 3 5 7 9 10 8 6 4 2

Verso
UK: 6 Meard Street, London W1F 0EG
US: 207 East 32nd Street, New York, NY 10016
versobooks.com

Verso is the imprint of New Left Books

ISBN-13: 978-1-80429-194-8
ISBN-13: 978-1-80429-196-2 (US EBK)
ISBN-13: 978-1-80429-195-5 (UK EBK)

British Library Cataloguing in Publication Data
A catalogue record for this book is
available from the British Library

Library of Congress Cataloging-in-Publication Data
A catalog record for this book is available
from the Library of Congress

Typeset in Sabon LT by Hewer Text UK Ltd, Edinburgh
Printed and bound by CPI Group (UK) Ltd, Croydon CR0 4YY

1
Cause and Affect

> *Did something happen and did I, because I didn't know how to experience it, end up experiencing something else instead? It's that something that I'd like to call disorganization, and then I'd have the confidence to venture forth because I would know where to come back to: to the prior organization. I prefer to call it disorganization because I don't want to ground myself in what I experienced—in that grounding I would lose the world as it was for me before, and I know that I don't have the capacity for another one.*
>
> —Clarice Lispector, *The Passion According to G. H.*

Art does not change the world. Sorry. Not in the way we sometimes hope it could. Not in the way we were told it would. Because what exactly *is* change? The mechanical action of cause and effect, in which an avalanche rolls down a mountain, a glass shatters into pieces on the concrete floor, or an airplane thrusts forward through the sky, does not seem to have a role in art. But if you were involved with art and progressive politics in the 2010s and 2020s you might have believed otherwise. During this time, many of us were more politically disorganized than we might have been before—overcome, perhaps, by a sense of disbelief that working in these established structures would change anything. Certainly, we are now more politically disorganized than is good for us. Our participation in trade unions, political parties, and other traditional political organizations plummeted, inversely proportional to our use of corporate-owned social media platforms as amplifiers. These platforms—with their monetization of attention and network connection—taught us something about disorganization that no political party membership could. Then came the crises of the 2010s and 2020s, which politicized the platforms but did not foster a structural breakthrough in getting us organized. "Hyperpolitics" is a term that the Oxford political theorist Anton Jäger has coined to describe this moment: everything becomes saturated with politics, but the planned, strategic political action we need does not happen. Sociologically, Jäger claims, hyperpolitics "is rooted in a society in which exit options abound."[1] It points at a fleeting sense of instability in getting political alternatives organized at scale, especially in comparison to the ascent of internationally coordinated right-wing populist, far- and extreme-right, antiliberal, and neofascist political organization that has been so typical of recent times.

The political theorist Chantal Mouffe once told us that she didn't want to use the term "political art" because it implied that "nonpolitical art" also exists. Mouffe's work—some of it developed together with her partner, Ernesto Laclau (1935–2014)—looked at reviving leftist thought and practice during a previous period of ideological crisis. That period is sometimes referred to as "post-politics," and Laclau and Mouffe saw it coming as early as 1985, when the power of classical Marxism had started to wane. They argued for a "new left" that would rejoice in the "infinite intertextuality of emancipatory discourses in which the plurality of the social takes shape."[2] Linked with the rise of New Labour in the UK in the 1990s and generally with the European political constellation after the fall of the Berlin Wall, post-politics was a hegemonic formation replacing the legitimacy of disagreement—for instance, between socialism and capitalism—with a form of technocratic management. It paved over the core ideas and the irresolvable contradictions of the social domain. Its adherents cosplayed that, in effect, "the political" was over, and maybe this is what they genuinely believed. Accepting that disagreement is fundamental to political life, Mouffe wondered how "conflict" could "be accepted as legitimate and at the same time take a form that will not destroy the political association, I mean, a form that will not be an antagonistic one?"[3] In hyperpolitics, then, the dissolution of the political association already seems to be a fact. It is precisely because no more association is permanent that everything else must compensate for this, including art.

If you lived in these times, you may have frequently read that art "changes the world"—for example, in a news article, press release, or exhibition announcement. If you think that this was something fringe and radical, well, the World Economic Forum championed it in 2016. If corporate donors tell you that your activist art is world-changing, and that's why they'd like to buy it, that could mean two things. Either they really love it (which is genuinely possible) or they need it because it might give them additional legitimacy during the contingency of hyperpolitics.

This book is not a critique of the art market. But the branding of "art as change" has become a corporate ceremony, or rite, that uses two key currencies—money and attention—shielding those who control key resources from being criticized themselves. Because who could be against something as vague but promising as "change"? While absent from Thomas Piketty's work on structural inequality, *Capital in the Twenty-First Century*, the art market "has become an excuse for banking in public," as one art dealer put it to the *New York Times* in the 2010s.[4] Aside from its upturns and downturns, the market is driven almost entirely by the currency of attention. The monetization of attention is also a key driver of what the critic and writer Anna Kornbluh describes as the "demand for either affirmation or cancellation," a binary that is now associated with hyperpolitics. The "flatness" of this arrangement is crucial, contends Kornbluh: "When presentation is personalization, when all content is self, when experience trumps idea, any dimensionality, ambivalence, or ambiguity disappears. As a result, tension and contradiction are excluded; only opposition remains."[5] Interpretation of works of art is everybody's business. But when done by a powerful backer or buyer, it can mean that a certain explanation comes to prevail over others and, moreover, that it blesses that backer or buyer with some of it. A 2020 working paper by the London School of Economics critically found that the "omnisignificance" of contemporary art, cited as "its ability to change meaning based on interpretation," was the key factor in this. And that should mean that works of art depend on perception and are thus proxies for navigating a form of uncertainty. That very aspect of art perception "seemed, in a world absolved of certainties, to enable art to act as a 'positional good' for the super-rich without forfeiting a posture of critique of the capitalist system of which it is part."[6] Okay. So in that kind of obvious, quasi-causal manner, art has not changed the world. Not yet. We stand by it. Let's, for the time being, not talk about cause and effect, but about cause and *affect*. Art makes us perceive, feel and sometimes even understand. What's the future of that?

Obviously, expediting artworks around the world to fairs and biennales causes art to impact the planetary environment and the climate. That is a kind of change. But it is no fault of art's own that it oftentimes has volume and weight. So this kind of environmental impact isn't an effect of art but more an affect of carrying it around the world. Selling and buying art also sends lots of cash around the globe. Or cryptocurrency, for that matter. That is also a form of measurable change. But people pay money for all kinds of different things, for supercars and microwave ovens and designer drugs and luxury showers. So the financial transaction isn't unique to art. The real cause and affect of art happen somewhere else, and in some other way.

A big question for this book is what that word "real" even means. At the start of this chapter, the protagonist of Clarice Lispector's novel thinks about what it means to live in reality.

From the stillness of her Rio de Janeiro penthouse, where she is about to have a life-changing encounter with a cockroach, G. H. expresses her desire to be in the world as it was before she had experienced it. Experience was a "grounding" that would make her "lose" the world as it was. Cockroaches have been around for 320 million years. So they are, perhaps, legitimate pointers to a world before human experience. But along the way, Lispector summarized what art is for. Art is the engine, or the organ, or the thing, or the verb, or the principle, that awakens our capacity to perceive anew.

Art must do *something* if it is to affect the world and our existence at all. If art were not to cause anything, the world would be the same without it. And the world is different with art than without it. This is because all art, across its many forms, media, and meanings, is similar in one aspect. That aspect is its *perceiver-dependence*. Art is an expression that invites somebody's perceptual and cognitive efforts to take part in its making of the real.

This is, at once, a reason art has become fundamental to the social and cognitive world and at the same time an explanation for why it is less directly efficient as a force of change than we may hope for. Being dependent on being perceived builds vulnerability into art that affects what it can and cannot do.

Art has, it seems, been culturally distinct in its involvement and exploration of perception as much as it has been socially distinct in its capacity to complicate it. Art is channeled through the same sensorial and neural systems that we use to process everything else. Art experience is tied up with all kinds of other events in the brain and the world. The fact that art can make us feel things that seem *better* and *other* than the real world does not imply its separation from it. Art reaches those who feel for it. Those whose perception wants it. Those whose inclination anticipates it.

•

Art commands and inhabits its own kind of silence—a quietness that has no equal in culture. The work of art is, as John Berger used to say, "silent and still."[7] It instills a world akin more to listening than to speech. Being perceiver-dependent is more than being subject to an aesthetic taste or moral judgment. It implies that perception itself is the thing that art wants and is about. And how perception works and evolves remains a vital question for art that reaches far beyond optics and aesthetics.

So, does art act in and on the world or not? This is a dilemma at the core of today's fraught moment in social relations, geopolitics, ecology, and cognition. It is a question that is less about what art does and more about what our perception does to it. How to go about this? What our perception does to art is co-decided by what else we find important besides art. What you love. The world. The world that loudly and urgently overwhelms any silence.

Perceiving art is coping with the uncertain. It is acquiring literacy about uncertainty. Art helps us understand something fundamental about our relationship to the external world: that we relate to it through our senses in a way that is messy and always requiring recalibration. No individual artwork can encode this relationship uniquely and forever. But art *as a whole* is an endeavor that sustains the link between *having* perception and *teaching* perception something about itself.

In order to go there, we ask the question what art is. And it doesn't want to be asked this question. Art evades direct interrogation. Obviously we can talk about what art is in a more technical sense, like how to make a drawing or a painting or a video, but the technical side doesn't reveal too much for now. When art "genres" are born—one artist sees another working in a certain way and emulates some of that approach—mostly technical or surface aspects are copied, not the part that's actually the art. You can look at thousands of "Cubist-style" images.

These patterns may hold information. But among thousands of "Cubist-style" images you may find nothing like art.

So, what is art? One type of answer can be gained by putting together a list of all the kinds of things, objects or actions, that can be art. Paintings, sculptures, musical compositions, videos, performances, pieces of silence, dust, bananas taped onto walls, exoplanets renamed, and so on. *Anything* that an artist nominates to be art also *can* be art. Say we thus complete the list. Soon after this goes to print, someone nominates something new to be art. The list is now incomplete. While forms art can take are important, they do not contain a limit and thus cannot really ever give the information we want. Instead, art is structurally perceiver-dependent. Art is somehow *completed* by the act of perception. Art is a form of culture that asks—time and again—to work out what it is that we perceive and what that tells us about *how* we perceive. And perception cannot be separated from cognition. In humans and nonhuman animals, perception is turned into experience by the mind's curation of sensory input.[8]

Imagine you are perceiving something without filtering it. It is what G. H. wanted. You are experiencing with sensorial input running "free," unconstrained from expectations built by prior experience. This would be called "bottom-up" perception. Sensations are (for now) unfiltered by most prior norms and constraints that are meant to delimit, organize, conceptualize what you experience. The incoming data streams are (for now) mostly ungoverned by predictions.

Going in the opposite direction, "top-down" perception reorganizes and compresses incoming information immediately. *Concepts* arise. The two streams interact constantly, so it's not like you're experiencing exclusively one of them in either direction. It is always both at the same time. In a top-down process, you can recognize your loved one by seeing only the tip of their nose and nothing else. Concepts like "nose," and "[the name of your loved one]" allow you to skip *a lot* of incoming sense data. You do not need to experience *everything*. Compression is real. What we compress, we reduce. What we reduce, we name. What we name, we instrumentalize. Compression is political for this reason: it lets us take something for granted. And in this precise grain of reality that we take for granted may have resided the overlooked. We're saying "overlooked" and not, for example, "unexpected," because not everything that's important stands out at first sight or impression. This is why the work of attention is so central for art, and it's also what's nerve-racking about it. Sometimes our inclination to perceive top-down makes us categorize, abbreviate, and compress *before* we have had a chance to sense. But art urges perception to let go of some of the presets and priors, increasing the cognitive work, activating more rather than fewer mental states. Experiencing is precisely not-knowing. Art is complicating the hierarchy between bottom-up and top-down perception. Art is, thus, a model for how reality remains new to somebody.

In visual art, the interdependencies of bottom-up and top-down processes are known as the "beholder's share." The term was coined by the art historian Ernst Gombrich. The beholder's share is the part of an object that happens in the mind of the beholder, making that object dependent on perceptual and cognitive processing. The beholder's share could not exist without something in the world to perceive. Let's call it the *work*. Likewise, the work could not exist *as art* without the beholder's share. Though it is not clear, therefore, exactly where the partition of perceiver-dependence takes place, it appears to be quite a solid prediction that art's significance to someone hinges on that partition having happened. It is like an internalized version hinting at the importance of interiority in general for art, the importance of processes that are outwardly invisible. Art is an act of faith in the work that its perceivers do below the surface. For Gombrich, this inner share was a foundational quality of art. The beholder's share goes for any work of art that you may be perceiving and for any way you may be perceiving it. It states that the perception of art creates a share of the art—a conscious experience of sorts—that is shaped by the perceiver's dispositions.

While this is the case for reality at large—we create an inner share of what we perceive *in general*—art further explores and complicates this process. Art sometimes seems *dedicated* to this aspect of perception.

It was surprising to us, although it should not have been, that there is a strong connection between Gombrich's beholder's share and contemporary cognitive science. The nineteenth-century physicist Hermann von Helmholtz is often regarded as a main forerunner. Helmholtz's notion of "unconscious inference" captured many elements of top-down perception, sensing that our perceptual systems process what they perceive using predispositions or mental models—adaptable presets, likely stored in the cerebral cortex of the brain. Contemporary neuroscientists follow up with experimental research that appears to confirm Helmholtz's ideas. For example, Anil Seth writes that "perceptual, cognitive, affective, and sociocultural expectations conspire to shape the brain's 'best guess' of the causes of sensory signals."[9] While the beholder's share exists not just for art but also for external reality in general, art may be specifically exploring this same "best-guessing" as a form of culture. And yet, all this guessing and adjusting goes so fast that we're barely conscious of it. How does art even intervene?

For many cognitive scientists, the external world we perceive is a creation of our minds to a much greater degree than we colloquially assume. There is talk of perception as a "controlled hallucination"—bringing the intuitions of Helmholtz and Gombrich to their ultimate consequences.[10] This is how psychologist Chris Frith specifies what's going on:

> Our brains build models of the world and continuously modify these models on the basis of the signals that reach our senses. So, what we actually perceive are our brain's models of the world. They are not the world itself, but, for us, they are as good as. You could say that our perceptions are fantasies that coincide with reality.[11]

If all perception happens under the influence of priors, art explores and complicates the models that we hold. Perception matters, for instance, for the question *where art begins*. It forces us to ask things like: Is there a proper boundary between simply perceiving something and perceiving something like art? Does art automatically begin once commonplace interpretations for a cultural "signal" have been exhausted? Or is this an entirely *mistaken* way of framing the question? Maybe art requires interpretative work that complicates the integration of perceptual and cognitive faculties. Maybe art is a qualitative interruption, a sociocultural vessel, for perceiver-dependence.

Two perceivers can agree that an object in front of them is a painting hanging in the stairwell. From there, differences branch out. For example, what does it show? And is it beautiful? On what evidence is such a snap judgment based? What makes that judgment? What does the work say about the world in which it was made and from which it emerged, and does that matter? We plunge into the domain of perceiver-dependence but also social and historical context. Observer-dependence exists most vividly in the active work that an observer does to process what they perceive. Art *depends* on perception.

Art is about getting your attention. But it shares your attention with things directly, physically important to survival. Art shares a space of attention with grocery shopping and price inflation and tsunamis and genocides. Living in a time of urgency changes perception. Being at the center of urgency, even more.

You can't restore a painting while gasping for air. You can't get around a drawing while you're being bombed. You can't concentrate on a "nonpolitical art experience" if your world is on fire. Debates ensue about which parts of the world are not yet enough on fire for that "nonpolitical art experience" to persist. And, of course, making that kind of geographical divide is faking the idea that you can structurally limit your field of awareness to only those things in your immediate surroundings and of your immediate interest, and leave out the rest. The story of perception goes differently, though. Perceiving art happens in a world of which our awareness seems ever more saturated. The situation rearticulates the necessity of art-making and art experience in times of urgency. But it also further endangers the time and space that can be afforded to art. Art needs the attention before it can give anything back. So talk about art as a "gate" to another world or future—as the writer Timothy Morton puts it—may be on the right track in some way.[12] But if you don't have the time or space to pay attention, you won't find that gate. You may not even know there was one.

For journalist and liberal news anchor Chris Hayes, we are living in an age of "attentional warlordism."[13] In *The Sirens' Call* he writes the history of attention as a history of American society and its media, and thus of their decline. That is, the decline of the printed newspaper, the vinyl record, and the video rental store. The decline, in other words, of some remnant, symbolic form of shared world, some kind of public square, a nostalgia for collective focus. The internet is first a source of hope until it too becomes toxic. Recommendation algorithms take over the experience of the open web, and our smartphones become dopamine machines, gluing us forever to the feed. Yet Hayes begins with an observation of his six-year-old daughter's "uncorrupted and pure" attention. Her "sweet, soft breath is on my cheek," he writes,

> as she cuddles up with a book, asking me to read it to her before we walk to school . . . There is nothing in this life that is better. And yet I feel the instinct, almost physical, to look at the little attention box sitting in my pocket. I let it pass with a small amount of effort.[14]

If this kind of attention exists and is worth fighting for, how do we ever *get* distracted and instead end up writing scores of books about our phones, social media, and attentional warlordism rather than about things we want and love? It shows the drama of modern attention through failing to write about what it is that you want and love. Maybe you start out writing about what you love but end up writing about—and thus giving more attention to—what distracts you from loving it more.

And yet, even when you are a paid worker of the attention industry, there seems to be something quite incomplete about the dichotomy that was just shown to us: that between an idealized, undivided attention versus push notifications on a phone. As a phenomenon deeply entwined with hyperpolitics, social media have come to play into our need for being validated and recognized by others—in an abstracted way, because many of these other inhabitants of attention-capitalized social fabrics are users we don't really know. This is something quite distinct from "screen addiction," or maybe it is a factor that plays into the *metrics* of attention. Your social media "likes" and other so-called virtual appreciations give you "real" doses of dopamine—the primary neurotransmitter linked to addiction. It gets released along specific neural pathways in the brain when we experience rewards, such as food, clothing, shelter, or a sexual partner, as Anna Lembke explains.

> Social connection has become druggified by social-media apps, making us vulnerable to compulsive overconsumption. These apps can cause the release of large amounts of

> dopamine into our brains' reward pathway all at once, just like heroin, or meth, or alcohol. They do that by amplifying the feel-good properties that attract humans to each other in the first place.[15]

Mass AI, in turn, adds intelligent interaction with machines to the dopamine mix. AI chatbots are 24/7-available conversation partners entering the sphere of social connection. Like "likes," they mostly tell you yes.[16]

Drawing on the affirmative bias of chatbots, the journalist Jamie Bartlett warns about the impact these models will have on their users' political choices. Elections, Bartlett says, will increasingly be decided by isolated voters talking to AI, looking for confirmation.[17] It makes one think that in this way, AI could further absorb what was left of political organization after hyperpolitics. One fervent user is the former British Prime Minister Boris Johnson, who intimated to the Saudi government channel Al Arabiya English that he writes entire books using ChatGPT, the popular chatbot. Johnson cheered: "I love AI ... I love ChatGPT ... it always says 'your questions are clever' ... 'you're excellent.'" The sixty-one-year-old then stumbled toward an inadvertent own goal: "I see great promise in this technology. Because ... human beings ... looking after the elderly costs an absolute fortune."[18] Technologies of attention have become emotionally integrated into the lives of many in the West, to the point that addiction to them outweighs the cognitive leveraging that AI may or may not provide. So the push notifications that keep us from focusing are the carrier signal of the politics of attentional warlordism—yes, to an extent. But some of these prompts represent real events—inconvenient, but real. Whether that's a distraction from nonpolitical art or a message in a bottle to the world depends on where you are in the story, whether you are merely perceiving or whether you are being materially affected. Hyperpolitics aside, this co-depends on things like geography—one of the rare features of the planet that stay rather motionless under the blanket of information. Geography is where people's exit options don't abound.

So it's somehow extra-offensive when art—or its celebration—disregards the bombing that's going on at the other side of the shared timeline. Disregards the people that are suffering and the population being further subdivided into those who do the partying and the posting and the celebrating and the selling, and those who do the dying. Such art—no matter how brilliant or smart or beautiful it may be—disregards, and in some sense offends, something that is central to our interdependent perception of the world today. The task for art to provide glimpses of joy and the glow of consolation becomes more central as the ability to experience that joy and to have consolation become more interdependent with the world itself. This idea of a brain that needs to hold many parallel realities in mind and figure out in what way to pay witness or enact solidarity articulates a problem that art has, probably, always faced in some form.

The ruins of the Gaza Strip, in Palestine, are visible from space. We look at a photo of the remains of Khan Younis. The entire area was leveled by the Israeli military in an extended killing spree. As of November 25, 2025, 72,500 Palestinians have been killed in an ongoing Israeli retaliation for an attack on civilians by Hamas on October 7, 2023, that cost the lives of 1,219 Israeli citizens and led to 251 hostages taken that day. The razing of Gaza showed a completely unhinged, unchecked military and state power, held back by nothing or nobody—and especially, by no moral or multilateral frameworks.

Among the ruins of Khan Younis, two Palestinian children walk with a large plush comfort animal between them. Its floppy ears betray that it is a dog. We must consider what else these children may still have left besides the object held between them as their joint possession. The landscape the two children are walking in, their home, is the absolute and bitter anti-image of the art world's abundance. As the world is moving from imperfect multilateralism to being dictated by the normless rule of brute force, to be able to continue any spectacle of arts and culture, everyone is kindly requested to look the other way.[19]

In 2025, the artist Jumana Manna unveiled *Sebastia*, a large public sculpture in Oslo. It is an elaborate street pavement made of leftover, rejected stones. The work is built, as Manna explains, from the ruins and the rubble of the Norwegian state. *Sebastia* is a scattered pattern of fragments from "demolitions, renovations and histories of roadworks, prisons, schools, tax offices, factories, dams, bridges, walls, saunas, royal plinths, roundabouts, and so much more," writes Manna. "For those of us born into ruination, the act of repurposing these ruins asserts an ecology and politics that resists disposability and acknowledges that we share our destiny with the lands that nourish us. To make something dignified and beautiful out of what remains has become our tradition."[20]

So art does create change after all. A tiny change. Every act of creation and every act of perception make the world into something different from what it was before, like cells renewing in our bodies. *Sebastia* is made of such cells too. If you were to describe the world with or without the art, you would not be twice describing the same world. The beholder's share is a good place to account for that subtle shift in what the world becomes with art: it adds not only material but also mental states, *brain states*, to the equation. Categories like *art made with technology*, *art by your ten best friends*, *art made in the last twenty years*, *figurative painting*, *Italian art*, *post-war minimalism*, *relational art*, *zombie formalism*, *post-internet art*, *decorated napkins*, and so on, dissolve under the condition of the beholder's share.

Neurobiologically, it might be neurons "firing" from the first encounter, so perceivers "store" works of art partially, fragmented, like an indefinitely incomplete portion of a cake. Over the many centuries that art has existed, we've grown used to this system working quite well. But from the way that art has evolved we might also grasp that our way of intuiting about it has no predefined boundaries.

The boundaries of art, if any exist, are the boundaries of perception and cognition. As they move, art moves with them. The times in which we are living ask us to feel more and understand more at the same time. In this way, one might say that *cognitive futures* emerge—possible futures of art (in the plural) that emerge by the shifting boundaries of intuiting, mentalizing, measuring, and modeling.

Here is a brief overview of the following chapters. "Carved Diagonals" talks about perception, cognition, and a hypothesis about an undivided proto-art typology that emerged 100,000 years ago or more. In the third chapter, "Useful User Illusions," we engage in a brief discussion of the notion of conscious experience. In "Abstraction," the fourth chapter, we ask whether deeper-level descriptions of art or its patterns can be modeled to make art—eventually—predictable by artificial intelligence. In chapter 5, "Mirror Neurons," the nineteenth-century history of the concept of empathy is traced through its origins in art. It continues with the discovery of the neuron and, much later, mirror neurons. In chapter 6, "Unknown Others," we look at the proliferation of empathy—and backlashes against it—in the twentieth and twenty-first centuries. "Don't Sacrifice Blue," chapter 7, asks whether and how art relates to climate change, geoengineering, and complex systems. The eighth chapter, "Transitional Objects," is about children and their plush toys. "Topsy-Turvies"—chapter 9—engages absurdist children's poems and intuitive physical models of how the world works. Building on this, the tenth chapter, "Poets and Particles," sets out with poetry, quantum mechanics, and the ordinary language in which quantum mechanics landed, all initiated by an AI-written haiku. The final chapter, "Non-Narratable Worlds," continues about the possibility of art in "non-narratable" quantum situations. There are physical situations in which we intuit that no art is possible—not yet, at least in our current understanding of it. But can art eventually emerge in these kinds of abstract physical configuration spaces for reality? If you could demonstrate this either way, you would be able to show that art can emerge only in certain descriptions of reality and not in others, or—conversely—that art can somehow exist in (or with) spaces other than those engaged by everyday physics and perception. We were reminded of the artist Robert Barry's 1969 installment of radioactive chemical elements in art spaces. Barry included a mention of the element's half-life into the work description, giving it a time base. Barry showed that these elements can function as art by creating a mental space—or a beholder's share—for them. What might possibly be built next on this legacy? Such a question belongs with an inquiry into the physical and cognitive boundaries of art that this book aspires to deal with.

Art is its own domain in the human world. But is it unique *to* the human world? That question belongs with the idea of cognitive futures, as it opens to the possibility that other species may share not just the practice of culture but, potentially, the making of art with us. A murmuration of starlings, for example, is an *emergent* system: a swarm for which the unity of all the birds together, perceived as a single entity, has become more than the sum of its parts. There is presently no conceptual bridge to view the murmuration as art, other than that it may feel like art *to us*. If we wanted to potentially find something like art in the animal world—or, for that matter, in nonhuman systems in general—it would have to be art *for them*. Baya weaver birds, found across the Indian subcontinent and Southeast Asia, create intricate, sculptural nests using plant fibers. Satin bowerbirds typically adorn their bowers with blue objects, creating a monochromatic yet complex form of attention-grabbing decoration.[21] These examples may look and feel like art to us. Again, a higher benchmark for art is introduced when we ask whether it is art *for them*, and how we could find out. Maybe we need to consider "art" outside of the aesthetics of nests and courtship rituals, and think of it as being reconfigurable within complex communication systems. Given the existence of these systems in animal societies, it would ask us to find some kind of demarcation between "ordinary" communication and "art," a distinction that is actually quite hard to draw if you think about it.

In the early 1970s, the Canadian American animal rights activist Paul Watson was confronting a Soviet whaling fleet near the Californian coast. Blasting a Zodiac over the water, Watson and his companion, the camera operator Fred Easton, looked on as a Soviet harpooner fired into a group of whales. Consequently, a wounded sperm whale surged toward them. They were astounded. As the *New Yorker* reported, the two prepared for the whale seeking a head-on confrontation.

> "It scared the hell out of us in the beginning," Easton said. "I just remember Paul saying, 'Here he comes!,' and we sat there. I couldn't get my camera going, and we both sat at the edge of the Zodiac, on the other side of which the whale was approaching. He swam right past us, and I swear to God he couldn't have been any more than ten feet away, and he was a huge male sperm whale, and he had an eye about the size of a dinner plate, and he did look at us with some sort of compassion, in the sense that he was certainly capable of doing harm to us in the circumstances, and had he been human we might have expected him to." The two men, watching the whale swim away, were overcome with emotion. "In an instant, my life was transformed

and a purpose for my life was reverently established," Watson later wrote.[22]

Easton's sighting of a "sort of compassion" seems significant for a changing attitude toward cetaceans. In 1970, biologists had released recordings of humpback whale vocalizations as a mainstream pop album. The long-distance "song" of humpback whales shared an epic, emotional character, making listening akin to experiencing an enigmatic lament from deep space. In a sense, *Songs of the Humpback Whale* brought about an early comparison with art. The album also propagated the movement to end commercial whaling. On the other hand, the whale's "compassion" can be seen through the lens of social neuroscience, especially through the concept of empathy that took hold in the late nineteenth and early twentieth century. Easton intuiting this is a form of cognitive futuring.

But let's think about the humpback whale vocalizations. Once you call these "songs," that's like calling them music. In a sense, you're calling them art. But you haven't figured out yet whether or not it is music (or art) *to the whales*. There is no way yet to ask a whale-led social world that question. Hence, the "song" label said very little about what was going on. Indeed, the vocalizations may be *culture*. The social and cultural lives of whales seem to form an important reason or context for their vocalizations.[23] Humpback vocalization involves distinct acts of singing and listening on the part of the whales. The philosopher and musician David Rothenberg has proposed that humpbacks "sing *for* each other, not *against* each other."[24] Researchers said they have detected *informational hierarchy* in humpback whale vocalization, and even *recursive hierarchy*, which is a property of human language.[25]

The Dutch American paleontologist Hans Thewissen discovered that all modern whales are distant relatives of a small deer that lived in modern-day India and Pakistan about 50 million years ago. The missing link between this early whale (that lived on the land but likely retreated into water when it needed to escape predators) and modern whales is provided by the build and structure of their ear bones. A well-preserved tympanic bone belonging to an ancient small deer showed the unique features of a whale ear, involving a thickened bone called the *involucrum*, as well as an S-shaped bone called the *sigmoid process*—a delicately complex structure that has persisted in modern whales unchanged. Thewissen explains that, "for an anatomist, the ear makes the whale."[26]

Sperm whales are the largest of the toothed whales and the world's biggest predators. They also have the largest currently known organic brains. They communicate in their submarine environment with click-like vocalization patterns called *codas*. To the human ear, the codas sound like a kind of hyped-up underwater Morse code. Apart from the complex biomorphology of their vocalization, sperm whales have a relatively large brain area involved in auditory processes.[27]

So what are these codas? The "culturally defined, multi-level," and "matrilineal" societies of sperm whales have fed the hypothesis that their communication system must be of commensurable complexity. Coda learning may be some kind of inter-whale educational process. The relative simplicity of the clicks seems to contradict the "social and behavioral complexity" of the whales' lives, leading to the question of whether "any additional, previously undescribed structure" might be present in their vocalization patterns.[28] The researchers noticed that the silences between the clicks varied depending on context. This variable was termed *rubato*. Also, the animals were found to be sometimes adding an extra click to a previously known pattern. The extra coda was called *ornament*. We get the sense that the codas allow for some untapped expressive richness and variety. Maybe the whales are chattering, as if you suddenly found yourself in the pages of *Wings of Fire*, the young-adult fantasy book series full of constantly talking teenager-like dragons.

Then came a breakthrough finding that went beyond rubato and ornament. Focus lay on "spectral" properties—modulation of the frequency. Slowing down the codas revealed spectral properties—changes in tone. That idea arose when the computational linguist Gašper Beguš attended a lecture about elephant communication.[29] Maybe a sperm whale perceives the clicks at a slower rate than we do, processing them differently. And thus, the speed of the clicks could be seen as relative rather than absolute.

Beguš's intuition to slow down the codas shares an artistic intuition with, for instance, pianist, composer, and conductor Reinbert de Leeuw's early 1970s decision to play Erik Satie's *Gymnopédies* for solo piano at a much slower speed than customary at the time, revealing new properties of the music.

Rather than as simple clicks, the codas came to be thought of as "pulses," akin to the "glottalic pulses of human vowel production," wrote Beguš with Ronald Sprouse, Andrej Leban, Miles Silva, and Shane Gero. To investigate the codas, they used an artificial neural network that had previously been trained to discover meaningful properties in human speech without supervision. Seen in this way, the generative adversarial network (GAN) could be compared to a contrast-heightening operator on a digital picture. Without knowing what is depicted, the system highlights discernable points of interest that might otherwise stay overlooked, like mapping an abstract territory without yet understanding the landscape. The researchers found, within coda patterns that once had seemed to sound like monotonous clicks, the equivalents of human vowels.[30] The spectral properties confirmed the potential of the coda system to enable an enormous variety of learned expressions. The finding raises the stakes that the codas are a communication system that may reflect the complexity of sperm whale societies, in the way that language reflects ours. The authors note, though, that they don't know yet what the patterns might mean or refer to.

Suppose that the codas *are* a little bit like language after all. It is a matter of speculation to ask what could be communicated with such a system. Could the codas express interiority, or communicate feeling? Is it plausible that, for all the years that a sperm whale mom nurtures her young, some kind of interior report might be shared between them, or some kind of detailed affective message? For the codas, the "ornaments" taunt the vocal imagination as much as the typographic one. So, what would it take for something like *poetry* to emerge in a communication system like this? Most likely, a beholder's share. A way that it is poetry *for the whales*. A way, also, to appreciate the communication system's properties for their own sake. Poetry can be something like a *system check*. Not as in *hello, world*, but more like *hello, language*.

2
Carved Diagonals

A dialogue from the online language-learning game Duolingo introduces a dilemma that has bothered art perceivers for some time: how to discern art from nonart? It may seem here as if nothing in the observable world can be surely categorized as nonart:

NARRATOR: Eddie and his friend Oscar are at an art museum. Eddie looks at a painting of a dog.
EDDIE: This is my favorite painting in the museum.
OSCAR: That painting is boring!
EDDIE: What? I like dogs!
OSCAR: Eddie, I'm an art teacher. I know good art. This painting is not good art.
EDDIE: Why?
OSCAR: Good art is interesting. Good art is surprising.
NARRATOR: Oscar sees a sandwich on a chair.
OSCAR: That is good art!
EDDIE: A sandwich on a chair?
OSCAR: Yes, it's interesting and surprising! The artist is a genius.
EDDIE: I don't understand art.
NARRATOR: A janitor walks into the room. He starts eating the sandwich.
OSCAR: Excuse me, you can't eat the art!
JANITOR: This isn't art. This is my lunch.[1]

A sandwich on a chair can be art when it is intended to be so. Or when it is being looked at in some way. That is to say that, ultimately, art, like the external world, comes together in the acts of perception and the internal model of the art that these acts construct. This aspect of experience and perception, which art complicates, is expressed by Chris Frith: "Our conscious experience is determined by a combination of top-down processes (e.g., prior beliefs) and bottom-up processes (e.g., sensations). The balance between these two processes depends on estimates of their reliability (precision), so that the estimate considered more reliable is given more weight."[2]

The element of guesswork, and thus uncertainty, is important. It was the statistician Thomas Bayes (1701–1761) who first jotted down a quantitative notation of the balance between prior beliefs and incoming evidence, which today is variously known as *Bayesian inference*, *Bayes' rule*, *Bayes' theorem*, or even the *Bayesian brain*. It goes like this. Say we observe phenomenon A, about which we hold certain beliefs. These beliefs are the "priors." The act of perceiving A produces new evidence Y. How much should we update our knowledge of A, given the incoming Y?[3] The central idea of Bayesian inference is that perceptual and cognitive systems are always best-guessing from what is available to them. This introduces a sense of never reaching a conclusion. While no best guess is final, no final guess is perfect.

In recent times, Bayesian inference has become something of an operating paradigm for the cognitive world. As a way of thinking about best-guessing, it also has gained a strong footing in computational neuroscience and artificial intelligence. When, on August 19, 2024, the sailing yacht of the UK tech tycoon Mike Lynch sank during an unexpected storm near the coast of Sicily, the public caught a glimpse of this. Hinting at chanciness, Lynch had named his ill-fated vessel the *Bayesian*.

So, as one author puts it, "[Bayes' rule] affects us all. It's a logic for reasoning about the broad spectrum of life that lies in the gray areas between absolute truth and total uncertainty."[4]

The one-size-fits-all character of Bayesian inference has also led to critique. According to the psychologists Jeffrey Bowers and Colin Davis, "there are too many arbitrary ways that priors, likelihoods . . . etc. can be altered in a Bayesian model in order to account for the data that are obtained." Some Bayesian models, they argue, were even "built *post hoc* in order to account for the data."[5] The suspicion is understandable. In a sense, Bayesianism is too good to be true. It makes no commitments to what is actually the case, updating instead what we *infer* to be the case. So the Bayesian model—in which we're constantly best-guessing—is extremely flexible. It is totally on board with perceiver-dependence. Moreover, all the uncertainties that are encoded in art and its perception seem to have been already accounted for.

From a Bayesian standpoint, therefore, Eddie and Oscar each have their own priors. And that's okay! Eddie's is his love of dogs. Oscar's is his being an art teacher, which makes him, in his own eyes, an art expert. For Eddie, an object is great art when it has a dog in it. For Oscar the object has to be *surprising* to be art. That the object turns out to be the janitor's lunch highlights the material base of all of this. Not only artists but also janitors must eat. Museums could not exist without janitors and artists; their sandwiches are *historically materialist*.

Oscar's inference about the sandwich betrays a love for the twentieth-century "readymade." The readymade was defined in 1938 by the Surrealists as "an ordinary object elevated to the dignity of a work of art by the mere choice of an artist."[6] With the readymade, perceivers faced new questions about the boundaries of art. But these uncertainties were cushioned by the steady ascent of institutional gatekeepers in the art world. They kind of took Oscar's position: a sandwich can be art once an artist chooses to put it in the gallery. This, in fact, does more than confuse the game of definitions. The readymade in the museum is an institutional translation of the notion that art requires metacommunication (or communication about communication), that it isn't sufficient to simply have art as something unexplained and unnamed but that it, while elementary to human culture, needs an external framework, mode of discourse, or language to make sense of it. Imperfect as it is, today we have that framework. But how did it emerge?

What was, in human culture, a first externalized expression that tested bottom-up and top-down perception together? We don't know what it was, but we know it wasn't in an art institution. There weren't any yet. Nobody knows how this occurred, but we know that it must have happened at some point: the emergence of not just the art but also the wrapper around it—a kind of metacommunication that enabled us to perceive art as something distinct. Today, we have become completely accustomed to equating art with that which is officially called so. But more foundational qualities must underlie it, paving the path toward art. What are they?

The anthropologist Ellen Dissanayake has suggested that art is about "making special." This may sound quite right, since whatever art is or does is usually contrasted with something that's more ordinary and pragmatic, thus less special. But once we get to work on locating some cognitive, evolutionary, or other boundary between everyday and special, plain and bespoke, deadpan and boutique, things get tricky. Does such a boundary even exist? In some way, it seems like it does. A poem is, by its use of language to convey an idea, a point of view, or simply some specific *pattern*, a bit more "special" to us than, say, a grocery list. Specialness over the shopping list might stem from a poem's linguistic form and emotional content, on the one hand, and from its capacity to deviate from our expectation—to defy our predictions, to surprise us—on the other. That is to say that also a terrible poem can be surprising.

Though it feels quite right that art has something extraordinary to it, *special sauce*–style arguments—in which mysterious ingredients or effects are set apart from "mere mechanism"—don't hold much explanatory power, or at least that's how we feel about them.[7] Our point here is that art's "specialness" may not be sufficient to explain it. Specialness, after all, could be called "artness," by which we, yet again, would end up having no real explanation at all. Nevertheless, Dissanayake sensed how art is elementary to the *social* world. She wrote: "Social systems that disdain or discount beauty, form, mystery, meaning, value, and quality whether in art or in life are depriving their members of human requirements as fundamental as those for food, warmth, and shelter."[8]

This rings true, at least to us. Art belongs with things like food and shelter—the basics. But it can become critically endangered when food and shelter aren't in place. So this isn't about *special.* It's something else. There's something elementary to art, but how did that become so? If art is fundamental, does it have a physical substrate in us, just like we have a digestive system for the food we eat? Is the function of art somehow anchored in our bodies, our neurons, or brains?

Neuropsychologists are interested in these kinds of questions, but their findings are incomplete. In an attempt to locate art, neuropsychologists try to identify regions of the brain that are active during the making or perception of external aesthetic objects—not to say "art." In parallel, they are seeking biological and evolutionary explanations for art's emergence into the world. They are trying to map art to the brain as well as look at its emergence and its evolution over many tens of thousands of years.

The first finding appears to be that art lacks a clear, single locale in the brain. The second is that there is no rock-solid way to match or patch human evolution to early art expression. But there may be some clues.

In early human societies, art may have emerged before or along with language and the development of social complexity. In exactly what kind of order and arrangement this may have happened remains unknown, of course. But relationships with language as well as with social life seem to be important for art in general because both art and language respond to and record complexity. This is inherent when focusing on humans, who have language and art and complex social structures. But we need to imagine how these structures came into being conjoined.

An additional quality unites art with language: *externalization*. Since human mental states dating back 70 to 100 millennia are not accessible, we are looking at what remains of what was externalized and considering what they may be. Fair or unfair (probably unfair), in order to find art we look at what was externalized.

The emergence of art onto the human scene, hundreds of thousands of years ago, could be correlated with a simultaneous increase of complexity in both the neuropsychological interior and the social exterior of humans. The mind, and its external world, suddenly became more complex and multi-layered. Coincidentally or not, tools or technologies, or ways of using the body, became useful to enable externalization. These may well have been accompanied by a wealth of verbal and physical parallel expression that is now lost.

Scientific attempts to identify a dedicated "art system" in the human brain so far have been unsuccessful. They have yielded no results, in that there are currently no known regions of the human brain that exclusively cater to art. The brain regions that are "believed to sustain aesthetic experiences," writes one group of authors, "are involved in innumerable other kinds of experience. This suggests that artistic and aesthetic activities rely on nonspecific neural mechanisms, which might even be shared with some of our close primate relatives."[9] Though it sounds a bit impolite to call art a by-product of cognitive development, it might be something like that. It might be an initially unintended side effect or surplus that has taught us to perceive more critically and has become indispensable since.

Neuropsychology offers surprising findings about humans and visual expression. One of them is that oftentimes children who have been blind since birth can quite realistically draw objects from the surrounding world without ever having seen them. The fact that they can shows that the mind, when steering for visual expression, taps into other-than-visual-information to build the expression. For the neuropsychologist Dahlia Zaidel, this is possible because "representations of knowledge are organized through concepts, and need not depend on visual input alone."[10] Concepts can be used on a different level than only the sense data that were given to the brain.

Let's look at the object "bison." And let's look at what developmental psychologists call "object permanence." It means that when we see a bison and then don't see it (for example, because it has gone behind some trees), we *predict* that it's still there. But we can also look at object permanence as part of a broader cognitive evolution. Indeed, "the capacity for object permanence has been important in the evolution of language, in the stage before there was language."[11] So, if you can see the animal, whatever it is, and then you can't see it, you need to take something in mind—something that's *not* the animal—to continue knowing that it exists.

What is it? A concept? A prediction, expectation, best guess, or model? Something like a memory of the bison's very recent disappearance behind the trees? But how do you hold that memory without your actual sensorial input confirming that the bison is still there? Maybe you solve it, unconsciously, with a placeholder, a pointer, something that prefigures conceptual usage. A bison was there. And, although we can't see it for now, the pointer still points there.

We can imagine that the bison stays away for a bit longer than expected. We'll need something like a more solid internal symbol to project its permanence. We need something to be able to refer to it *tomorrow*. Indeed, a next stage of object permanence is *displaced reference*, which is an important feature of human language. The word "bison" can be used in the absence of an actual bison. It can function as a stand-in for the bison itself and function with no bison in sight. Displaced reference was long thought to be unique to humans, but chimpanzees and bonobos, for instance, have it too. They too are "capable of displaced reference to absent and displaced objects."[12] The point of words and names functioning more abstractly as *concepts* is that you can invoke them in the absence of their carriers.

While displaced reference is most frequently highlighted as a feature of verbal and written language, it is also a feature of art. A drawing of a bison also functions as an externalized, displaced reference that endures in the absence of the actual bison.

Red ochre pieces found in the Blombos cave in South Africa have shown engraved markings of up to around 100,000 years old, although instead of "found in" one might more appropriately say "extracted from." We don't want to suggest that an archaeological process by which some objects get privileged and appraised while others get discarded—like signal and noise—is without its own problems. Basically, to determine what a signal is, you have to make assumptions about what isn't. But if the entire reality—nature itself—were animated, spirited, then reality may have been already cognitive and full of signals, yet without producing the kinds of externalizations and objects—like the ochres—that we now "read" and treat as exclusive proof. So the ochre carvings are discovered, and they become part of a narrative that, with the advantage of hindsight, is reasoning toward a modern world. They become privileged, in that sense. Yet, on the other hand, they do seem to appear at one point in time and not at an earlier point, and so they *do* seem to provide evidence of a cognitive process for which no evidence was preserved before. The idea about progress that is embedded in this evidence is that *more* information is present, and that perhaps, with the carved ochres, a yet-unspecified symbolic notation on the edge of language and art appears to enter the scene. These are big hypotheticals derived from mere *traces* of a reality nobody can fully contextualize anymore. The Blombos ochres are weak signals of something we don't understand, signals of something that we might, at the same time, call *emergent*, in the sense that they seem irreducible to the previously known parts of the world they stem from.

They are much older than the oldest known cave paintings. They may signify a kind of dawn of modern cognition, as far as archaeological evidence permits us to say such things. The ochres—with diagonal lines forming lozenge shapes—feel a little like primordial Post-it notes, carrying scribbles. Is it proto-writing? Is it proto-counting? Is it proto-doodling? Even if the artists were only doing just that—doodling around with the ochres—a threshold has been passed. A significant cognitive leap was made. There is evidence of the externalization of a mental idea. Some researchers seem to consider the markings not language per se, and not art per se, but a yet-undifferentiated form of both. The Blombos ochres carry the oldest known "intentional images." They were probably made with "symbolic intent."[13] The engravings are graphic structures of lines. They don't resemble anything in particular, which makes them seem kind of multifunctional. Maybe they were used for displaced reference. Maybe they were an account of a buffalo hiding behind and appearing from the woods. Who knows? These engravings constitute "an external, abstract representation of internal high-order cognitive processes" that is similar to language.[14] The Blombos ochres, at the threshold of a complexifying cognitive world, show how symbolic, conceptual externalization—associated with both language and art—is still distinct from depiction, figuration, or full representation.

For Shigeru Miyagawa, Cora Lesure, and Vitor A. Nóbrega, they can be seen as proof of *some kind* of top-down cognitive process. Indeed, for these authors, "the symbolic thinking that developed in modern humans led to a fundamentally different way to compute data, one that extracts only the essence required for abstract representation instead of computing the entire set of incoming raw data ... [thus] the development of the arts gave the modern humans a powerful evolutionary advantage."[15]

This is a way of asking whether art changed the world when it first appeared. And it seems like it did. Consider the possibility that art emerged conjoined with language and, thus, strictly chicken or egg, with a kind of metacommunication about it. For the linguist Riny Huybregts, "taking symbolic behavior as a proxy for communicative language use, fixation of externalized language must have emerged around, say 100,000 years ago."[16] Then the Blombos ochres seem to support the idea of a co-emergence of art with language. In an article that dates the earliest language in modern humans at 135,000 years ago, Miyagawa and his co-authors build on Huybregts's points. They talk about the Blombos ochres art as "proxies for language, and not necessarily to have been preceded by it."[17]

Older even is a geometric engraving discovered on a fossil freshwater shell from Java, Indonesia. Dated at 400,000 BCE, the shell engraving places the kind of externalization that led to art much further down into the past, and—significantly—also ties it to a predecessor of *Homo sapiens*.[18] As a piece of evidence, the shell speaks to our attention for anything that's carved, anything that's like proto-symbolic notation, anything externalized that seems to point at a yet-undivided core of language, of art, of counting, of pattern-making. With the carving (or doodling) now being located several hundreds of thousands of years earlier on the timeline than the oldest previously known examples, the notion of a single advent of a single form of "modernity" becomes more doubtful. The emergence of a general cognitive state associated with modern humans may seem less linear than thought before. Perhaps that dawn of emotional and behavioral modernity could have been more like something flickering through deep time, initially conjoined with rather than radically separated from the cognition of nonhuman animals. Maybe that notion of modernity could be seen as something like an uncertain flame that was ignited several times before it became solidified in the branch of the world that we now inhabit. The carving is tied to the discovery of remains of *Homo erectus*—an early human—by the archaeologist Eugène Dubois. Dubois was stationed in Java in the late 1800s with the island's Dutch colonizers. Under their occupation, the entire collection of objects related to the discovery of "Java man" was shipped to Leiden. In 2025, the Dutch government announced the final return of the 28,000 fossils comprising the collection back to Indonesia.

Top-down inference is key to explaining art, but it also has its limits. If art were purely about the top-down process, it would be communicating much more efficiently than it does to us today. Visual art could come down to a kind of pictography or logo design rather than complicating perception. Instead, art is, or has become, more *complex* than strictly necessary for top-down communication. Artists control perceiver-dependence but cannot control it entirely. Perhaps art is mirroring the social world. Art makes us shuffle between upstream and downstream, rehearsing our capacity for perceiving anew.

For some researchers, "it is unlikely that there ever will be a unifying theory about art that would provide the starting point for a neurological top-down reduction."[19] Try all you want with art, but there's something missing if you just look at it as a way for concepts to efficiently go downstream—that's what the message seems to be. Instead, art has come to explore something that remains *inconclusive* between the bottom-up and top-down lanes of perception.

This inconclusive property of art perception may not have been initially obvious. But it is already there for us when we look at the Blombos carvings, the exact meaning of which we cannot decode. We may infer that symbolic intent is present but not what the carvings want to say. We fail to decode it and describe it instead as a small congregation of diamond shapes. This might be seen as a proxy for the idea that an element of nonunderstanding is vital to the experience of art. One might intuit that art—structurally—*only translates in part*, for otherwise there would be a more efficient way to say what needs to be said. The poet and translator Eugene Ostashevsky writes that "poetry is when you don't understand the language."[20] This too seems to point at the idea that top-down perception does not unlock all there is to art.

To our knowledge, the oldest currently known human-made figurative work depicts a buffalo. It's a 44,000-year-old cave painting from Sulawesi, Indonesia. The buffalo is part of a hunting scene. It has horns and an elongated body. Around it are human-looking figures bearing tails and snouts, though it is not known if everything was painted at the same time.[21] The buffalo is a discrete symbol that, in its isolation, appears to give credence to the top-down hypothesis. At the same time, speculations about more recent cave paintings have focused on the role that fire, shadows, and movement may have played in their making. Instead of picturing an animal from a preformed mental concept, in this thinking there were shadows—thrown on the rock walls by flickering fires—that accidentally resembled it. Tracing the shadows, the artist let the figuration emerge from a kind of randomness or noise. The art would have come about like seeing faces in the clouds.

There is no direct evidence to sustain this idea, of course. But Ernst Gombrich was into it nonetheless. He suggested that the artists in the cave were "to scan the vague forms of patches and shadows for the revelation of a bison."[22] Depiction emerged by scanning, guessing, faithful to what today is framed as Bayesianism. There's a concept in the mind—perhaps it is unaware of itself—and then a sudden throw of the dice matches that preference. If all this was indeed once happening on the walls of the prehistoric cave, then—according to one author—the artists were "reading figures into the rock forms that were not, strictly speaking, there," matching uncontrolled perception with a cognitive template.[23]

Then there was the case of the "macaronis," late Paleolithic finger tracings in clay that appeared on the walls and ceilings of limestone caves in France and Spain. These abstract markings were made with soft mud. With these formations looking fully abstract at first, to the French archaeologist and priest Henri Breuil it seemed that "people discerned parts of animals [in them] and realized that they could make pictures in this way."[24] In Breuil's thinking, the macaronis represented some kind of intermediate stage between random patterns and pictorial figuration, adding to the bottom-up hypothesis for art. So in this way we're going from shadows in the cave or mud markings on the wall to drawing and painting. A concept would make itself known to the mind by a kind of upward guessing until bottom-up and top-down streams settled on a temporary equilibrium: the depiction. This would be quite the way of drawing from nature—taken literally, as identifying imaginatively useful information from rock surfaces and random patterns. But is it plausible? Did it happen like that? Nobody knows. It is a hypothesis about the mixture of both data streams taking hold in art.

Art isn't special. It emerges out of cognitive evolution. With the social world, its externalization became more complex. Perceivers had to do more guesswork but also developed more cognitive tools for it. Possibly (and we don't know, of course), there was metacommunication about the externalization. Art likely began to perform specific roles and occupy specific positions in the societies in which it emerged. These, in turn, may have set it apart from the merely useful and functional qualities of everyday communication—in part because art involves bottom-up, sensing-first processes as well. All this doesn't necessarily mean that a visual artist had any kind of elevated status in society. A successful artist was an enchanter, maybe—but at the same time just as much a manual laborer in a league with blacksmiths and shoemakers, whose work, unlike most art, had an immediate use value.[25]

That is how we summarize it. But it doesn't say anything about meaning or beauty or feeling or emotion yet. Beauty is, still today, regarded as a key feature of art. Its perceiver-dependence is also society-dependence. The fact that art is part of a social domain implies that perceivers are influenced by the preferences of others around them, so that ideas around what is found to be "beautiful" are complex translations of wider sociocultural priors. These priors, in turn, are constantly challenged, even by some of the oldest-known human art. In retrospect, the buffalo on the Sulawesi cave wall has a definite beauty. Its concentrated presence, abstract like a dot, goes with the silence of the work of art that John Berger talked about. Its dignity in a cognitive world now gone is preserved, alive, by the art.

Works of art are strange islands of information that test how perception operates—sometimes critically so and always in the full, tangled mess of the world. So art, whether we like it or not, is cognitive and subject to cognitive evolution. If cognition changes, perception changes. If perception changes, art changes.

3

Useful User Illusions

What is it like to be you? The philosopher Thomas Nagel in 1974 proposed that "fundamentally an organism has conscious mental states if and only if there is something that it is like to *be* that organism—something it is like *for* the organism."[1] Decades onward, cognitive scientists and philosophers still sometimes use Nagel's criterion as a benchmark for conscious experience. Instances of there being *something it is like* for the organism amount to *subjectivity being real.* Whether or not subjectivity is *actually* real (in the same way that, say, gravity is real, or an electron is real) has remained a philosophical dilemma during all this time. But it seems that for art, it must be real.

The beholder's share is a mentalized partition of external reality that becomes "yours." That is, it consists of what a perceiver makes *their own* of a work of art—of *what it is like* for them to experience a particular work of art. In this notation, art seems to have no specific medium and no other objective than to procure, and in a sense maximize, this kind of experience.

So, imagine being before a work that truly arrests you. What are you actually experiencing? If you were to analyze it and reduce the experience to its ultimate physical sources, you might find matter, waves, and energy there. Photons bouncing off pigments that map to certain frequencies in the electromagnetic spectrum. Many of these physical interactions are not experienced consciously. For instance, the varying energy levels of the photons are known to us as colors.

Let's say that the work that arrests you is a painting. What does it show? Let's say that it's a painting of a dog, like Eddie's favorite artwork in the previous chapter. Does this painting show *just* a dog? Likely not. It is, at least, *some kind* of dog. Do you mean, like, a long-haired chihuahua? Yes, maybe. But also, the long-haired chihuahua has been painted *in some kind of way*. The painting has certain things going for it that make it noticeable, striking, loveable, beautiful. These aspects of the painting of a long-haired chihuahua have nothing to do with actual chihuahuas. They are the painting's qualities (not the chihuahua's). These qualities are picked up by you, a perceiver. To you they're figments of experience. Subjective experience is real for art. Or at least, that's what it feels like to us when we gaze at a painting of a long-haired chihuahua. And if we think about the experience in close detail, we may believe that it consists of smaller units or grains, like a composition being made of musical notes, in which each individual note has a distinct sense of *what it is like*.

Philosophers came up with a name for these figments. They've called them *qualia*. As the theoretical physicist Adrian Kent puts it, qualia are "individual sensation-components."[2] They're like a currency for qualities. What would an ice cream be without its taste? Qualia are the feels. They're a kind of internal notation for the feelings and impressions that we process. If so, then qualia don't seem to be about *agreeable* experience exclusively, like the taste of strawberry ice cream. Feelings of pain, for example, would be qualia. And pain is, perhaps, a bit more explicitly political than the tone of middle C or the redness of cherry red are—which we will try to explain. While music and color seem to count as pleasant figments of experience, pain, on the other hand, more sharply reflects the discrete position of an experiencer who can feel it while others don't. So, in a sense, pain detects and signals how an experiencer may become socially, culturally, ethically isolated. When pain becomes rationalized as something privy to its experiencer alone, we may be separating out the world in ways that could permit us to ignore any suffering that is not our own.

Countering this tendency, the author Sara Ahmed has theorized pain as a phenomenon that has the potential to open people to the "bodies" of others and, at the same time, as the very phenomenon that creates the impression of a "bodily surface." Ahmed's insights mirror those of the neuroscientist Antonio Damasio, whose work has long stood relatively alone in its defense of *feeling* as central to the cognitive and neurobiological functioning of even the smallest single-celled organisms. While Ahmed speaks of the bodily surface that gets perceptible through pain, Damasio mentions the boundary of the cell as a contained unit within which an organism measures its own well-being and internal valence, leading to an emergent sense of selfhood. Therefore, in both Ahmed's and Damasio's writings, qualia seem to matter, going against the grain of their dismissal throughout much of cognitive science. But as for qualia, again, they remain nonetheless conceptually imbued with some kind of faux rationalism that can feel misplaced given how hard it is to track what they even *are* or may be. Since pain is already feeling, why would we need qualia to say, basically, the same thing?

The term was coined in the 1930s by the philosopher Clarence Irving Lewis. Qualia are in no way like *things*, he argued. Here is where it gets confusing, because the singular of qualia is *quale*. This strongly suggests it *is* a thing—or a bit *like* a thing—of which there can be one or multiple, sitting in your mind like an individual, an atom: a thingy of subjective experience, isolated, examined. So qualia would be what you "get" if you tried to break down your conscious experience into smaller bits. But that's ridiculous. Because who says that you can deconstruct, for example, your impressions of a Hend Samir painting into individual packets of quality?

Samir uses a form of wavelike patterning from which figures and shapes emerge and into which they disappear again, making the works feel, at times, like oceanic movements or volcanic pits from which and into which figuration, event, and anecdote are dreamed or thrust into being. It is the waveform or glacier-form that carries the perceiving eye through a kind of roller coaster from one focal point to the next. By this method Samir invites perceivers to infer and wander. Some elements, traditionally called figurative, provide anchor points and focal concentration, whereas others assume a flow, carrying from one area of the work to another, affirming an underlying tableau-like organization of the painting.[3] The qualities always exist in combinations. So a look at almost any work of art shows the problem of the solitude of the quale. When, for example, looking at Samir's *Water Gun Game* (2023), isn't its blue-and-yellow combination a single quale, though it is comprised of at least two colors? Aren't the blue and yellow each their own quale as well, creating an *and-and* rather than an *either-or*?

Qualia feel like an attempt at getting foundational about experience, but it is unclear down to what foundation exactly. Whatever qualia are, they aren't like things or particles. According to Lewis, "they must be distinguished from the properties of objects . . . The quale is directly intuited, given, and is not the subject of any possible error because it is purely subjective."[4] So are qualia just words?

Whatever they are, *as words* qualia provide philosophical cover for the intractable relationship between experience and physicalism—the "explanatory gap" between our subjective experience and the foundational but largely imperceptible physical realities underlying them.[5] Physicalism, as Anil Seth puts it, is a worldview according to which "the universe is made of physical stuff."[6] Physicalism is like a supercharged materialism, without the sociopolitical commitments that once stemmed from its historical and dialectical variations. Instead, physicalists are adamant that there isn't anything but physics—which surely is one of the most ardently political things one can believe or say. Indeed, David Papineau asserts that physicalism is the name for "a particular kind of hegemony" that physical science has come to claim over other subjects.[7] When we're pressed to situate consciousness under this hegemony, we get that "conscious states are either identical to, or somehow emerge from, particular arrangements of . . . physical stuff."[8] These arrangements are the physical brain states, probably. They're what goes on in your brain while you have conscious experience.

When the philosopher David Chalmers coined an influential "core" to the consciousness dilemma in the 1990s, his stated belief seemed to be that you can't reduce consciousness to the known physical laws. Chalmers called this philosophical axiom the "hard problem of consciousness."[9] Maybe this sounds a bit like the hard question of art. If so, it may be a little similar to it in the sense that both problems, or questions, seem to look for some kind of hard-to-catch "core" of a phenomenon—consciousness or art—that is itself hard to pin down philosophically. But for Chalmers, the particular character of the hard problem of consciousness went down to the underlying physics. Even if you would have explained all of the technical elements, he claimed, the *conscious* part of it all would still remain at large. Chalmers illustrated his point with a thought experiment he called the "philosophical zombie." The living dead of cognitive science, philosophical zombies would show all the outward traits of conscious experience. But they would turn out to have no inner life at all if you cared to take a closer look. So they would demonstrate that you can have all of the external appearances of conscious states, yet none of the actual consciousness. Chalmers, a rock music enthusiast, even wrote and performed "Zombie Blues," a song visualizing the barren outlook of his philosophical creation.

So let's park that unsavory philosophical zombie for a bit and consider that we're interacting with nonconscious systems all the time *as if* they're conscious. We're projecting consciousness outward. When we're prompting an AI large language model and getting its perfectly nice conversational responses, we may be experiencing this as if we're talking with something *like* that outer simulation of consciousness that Chalmers had in mind. Instead of there being "consciousness" though, there's an artificial neural network. What used to be presumedly uniquely human language lives on, embedded, statistically weighed, as a mathematical reality inside the neural architecture, and gets resurrected by your prompt.

Some authors use AI models as their co-writers, companions, conversation partners—their co-zombies. And how about agent-to-agent, model-to-model conversations, online platforms on which talking AIs conspire together and humans are mere bystanders? Again it's nonconscious systems doing the talking and the listening. Also, your art, if not AI-generated, gets *seen* by AI; it's ingested, dissected, measured into "figments" of deep learning. AI sees AI—visual dialogues from model to model may lock out the human-made origins of the datasets and depart in unknown directions. Nothing like Nagel-style consciousness lives in these systems, yet they can perfectly act as if it does. So you've got something like a de facto conscious behavior of a system against a de jure consciousness that amounts to the realness of subjectivity.

So while there may be nothing it is *like* being a large language model, it talks as though there is. The material that the model ingested was made by humans and part of the games that humans play with their language. So there's an organic fact of the human experience that was transferred to the model as the way that this gameplay goes. This has primed the model to exhibit and rehearse a human mental feat that it doesn't actually have. Yet as models talk to other models, the incentive to simulate this humanlike de jure consciousness might erode, evolve, or transform.

If the hard problem of consciousness in organisms is real, it would be "inexplicable by the currently understood laws of physics," writes Kent.[10] This is seen as an extreme position in which consciousness is *strongly emergent* out of brain activity. It would imply that consciousness is in every which way more than the sum of its parts. It would be *more* emergent than the bird murmuration, in which a large group of birds seemed to interdepend, coordinate, and behave as a singular being.

Art is remarkably good at producing figments of experience—but there are no signs that it is inexplicable according to the currently understood laws of physics. Art is quite good at generating qualia. And "beholder's share" remains a useful name for their storage space. What this doesn't reveal, however, is how these impressions relate to the total number of one's physical brain states. To define qualia better we would need to find out to what physical brain states they map, or don't. There might be far more brain states than there are qualia. We need, as Kent puts it, "some sort of data selection principle" that could help explain how we get from all brain activity to qualia. He proposes that "the vast majority of the information encoded in a configuration space description of the brain's physical state does not appear to be carried by the associated consciousness." So, based on some sort of reduction, data would need be *left out* to get from brain activity to qualia.

Brain activity is signified by neurons "firing." Neurons—elongated nerve cells—are excited with small electric currents that, at a microscopic level, represent cognitive activity. Kent argues that with the brain containing "roughly 10^{11} neurons, firing on average roughly 10^{2} times per second, giving roughly 10^{13} discrete signals per second," and further down to the atomic level, a vast number of independent parameters—no less than 10^{78}—would be required to keep track of it all. He claims that this exceeds the "bitrate" needed to map our conscious mental states. Drawing what he calls a "cartoon" of the situation, Kent suggests that a far *greater* number of different brain states might map to a far *smaller* number of conscious mind states.[11] So, while qualia remain at large physically, they may have gotten us closer to an appreciation of *brain activity*.

Skeptics like the cognitive scientist and philosopher Daniel

Dennett have suggested that qualia are merely "user illusions." "That 'quale' of yours," Dennett wrote, "is a character in good standing in the fictional world of your heterophenomenology, but what it turns out to be in the real world in your brain is just a complex of dispositions."[12] In this view, qualia are by-products of brain activity with no bearing on the real world. But what exactly would such a by-product be? If you believe that everything is real *except* for your sensations, you are suddenly in a rather awkward conversation with art. That, in turn, feels like a kind of *foundational awkwardness* that has arisen between art and science. It is very specific when it comes to qualia: Can you still be an artist or art perceiver if you need to sign on the dotted line that your figments don't register on the physical map?

Kent appears to suggest that qualia should be weighed in relation to physical brain states, not in relation to the external world and involving many different forms of experience. So, indeed, if the amount of physical brain states far exceeds the number of qualia that report conscious experience—and someone would need to find out *how* the brain gets from one to the other—then we have approached the problem quite differently from Dennett. This direction seems to suggest that qualia *are* the reduction.

Maybe there is a benefit for art to trigger more qualia rather than fewer. Since the more qualia we get, the more brain states they map to, the more brain activity art induces overall. With this in mind, we can speculate about why it is that art has spread across culture and social space, taking on *any* form, medium, or material. Maybe, by sprawling all over the social world, art exercises an implicit advantage of sorts: to maximize qualia and thus brain states. Surely it does more with these brain states—to move, to make aware, to communicate, if not a message then a presence. The neurobiologist Semir Zeki writes that artists are "in some sense neurologists."[13] To the cognitive scientist Merlin Donald, art is "cognitive engineering."[14] All this may feel a little more plausible now. Yet what is art engineering for?

4
Abstraction

Two people are obsessing over a lute. The instrument is lying on the table. They've built a kind of bridge over it. A rope is strung over the lute, like a line, like a vector stretching to the vanishing point. The lute is a musical instrument that, due to its bodily proportions and curves, is hard to draw from most angles. So you need a technology of sorts to help you with that. A 1525 woodcut by Albrecht Dürer shows it at work. During this phase of transition in the visual arts, perspective was both discovered *and* invented. Objects represented in works of visual art evolved from semi-flat, ideographic signs to complex bodies in three-dimensional space, submitting to a scientific view that was seemingly brought in from without, since perspective worked quite independently from what a painting "meant." The advent of perspective, though commonly associated with naturalism, seems to contain an abstract take as well. A deeper-level idea of the nature of reality taking hold in art, perspective was both perceptual *and* cognitive. And if, at the time, you witnessed how it was changing art, it might have felt like a flatland was vanishing. From your local vantage point it may even have felt like this was a kind of endgame for art. Think of certain artists , like Dürer, as harbingers of technological license-holding. In this case, license holders of the new technologies of perspective. Maybe these technologies were a bit like what artificial intelligence in art seems to us today. Maybe AI is a bit like the lute that's changing our idea of art.

Technological innovations disrupt probability distributions. They change what you expect might be made next—sometimes perceptually, but at other times materially. Think of the pencil, for instance. The first currently known *drawing* was made with a pencil that was in turn made of ochre. A pencil, when used, leaves a trace on a surface. And it comes with an ethical question at the same time: What material is available and suitable enough so that we may waste it, spill it, and draw with it? In this way, a pencil is a question about material ground truth. Artists Raghad Saqfalhait and Mariam Dahabreh invoked it by creating a pencil from sawdust from Palestinian carpentry workshops, mixing it with pigments and a bio-binding agent.[1] A user is drawing with what was once considered rubble or waste. While Saqfalhait and Dahabreh's pencil disrupts the probability distribution in a different way than perspective did, both are ways of *designing for art*.

Today, AI and sawdust—perspective and pencil—speak to vast asymmetries in power, priorities, and access within art. They seem to think about the world so differently—and emerge out of such radically contrasting political realities—that they appear very difficult to reconcile. Is art, then, designing for a kind of material ground truth? Is it designing to transmit feeling, or thought? Or is it, rather, designing and engineering its own deeper-level, even *scientific*, description? We could also frame this in another way. Maybe technology is less about what kind of equipment artists get to play with, and more about the kinds of *underlying models* for art that this kit (or technology) is both informing and informed by.

If you were to frame art as a game with near-infinite possibilities and yet latent, implicit rules, that wouldn't be too far off. Think about the abstract strategy board game of Go, for example, as a game with near-infinite possibilities and *known rules*. The number of "legal" (that is, *valid*) board positions in Go is estimated to approach 2.1×10^{170}. It's an astonishingly large number, but a number nonetheless. The possibilities are, eventually, finite. Famously, the most advanced human player globally, Lee Sedol, in 2016 played five matches against an artificial neural network, AlphaGo. Lee lost four of them to the AI. The battle is considered a watershed moment in the "deep learning" phase of AI as well as for the game of Go. Famously, one of the AI's moves on the nineteen-by-nineteen board, known as "move 37," was so out of the ordinary that analysts thought it was a mistake at first, and definitely nonhuman in character.[2]

The game of Go feels artlike through its combination of near-infinite possibilities *and* visual abstraction, which enables you to see things *through* those many possible moves. There are no hidden layers to the board. You're looking at the configuration space itself. Go's artlike-ness feels strong, for instance, when you look at the names that have been given to the many different moves and positions. On the website senseis.xmp.net there are many examples, such as "loot a burning house," "conceal a dagger in a smile," or "bamboo joint." Each name betrays shrewd strategizing and imaginative play. Every name summarizes a particular diagrammatic game constellation, so that these board positions, in turn, feel like ideograms: characters that are pictures. In that sense, Go seems to have a transdisciplinary quality between art, strategy, and math.

If computation is something like a foundational code for intelligence, which some of the leading voices in AI seem to believe, where does that situate art? The direct link between intelligence and computation is about the "development of functional complexity through predictive pattern completion."[3] This powerful idea targets, potentially, all phenomena and aspects of reality for which a configuration space can be modeled through a long series of best guesses. It potentially abstracts a lot of, well, "clutter" that belonged with an intermediate sphere: *culture*. Culture is (or was) a domain we held more or less in common. Culture is a pluralistic domain that holds *some of us* in common across different versions of a "we." Culture used to be a site in which we would encounter each other and the art between groceries, laundry, bus, taxicab, plumber, caregiver, cleaner, schoolteacher, museum janitor, music class, neighbor. And as the everyday material reality remains, with their subsumption under AI, some activities become readily abstracted—that is, they're effectively made part of predictive pattern completion.

Some forms of labor, though, remain stubbornly ground-truth materialist. South Korean designer and artist Si Weon Kim struck a chord about this in a tweet about laundry. The post, from her now-deleted account, read, "someone on korean twitter said why are AIs drawing when there are 50lbs of laundry to be done at home ... kind of true ... why am i hand-washing my panties why machines are making art ... idk."[4]

So, can art be fully captured under pattern prediction? Lee Sedol, the Go champion, decided to quit the sport, or the art, after AlphaGo took over. The details about Lee's resignation are significant. "The Go I learned was a form of art," Lee said in a 2024 video interview with Google Korea. Pre-AI Go was a cultural practice "where you think by yourself and through interaction between two people." However, playing against AlphaGo was very different. It was like playing tennis against a wall. A wall that played extremely well. It has changed the centuries-old sport forever. "The records of games before and after the advent of AlphaGo are completely different," Lee explains. "Now, they hold only historical value. In fact, they are no longer used to study Go."[5]

AlphaGo was designed by DeepMind—a UK-based AI laboratory that is part of Google. Its founder, Demis Hassabis, aims to "solve intelligence and then use it to solve everything else."[6] The phrasing of that ambition betrays, in philosophical terms, an underlying view that intelligence is substrate-independent—that it doesn't fundamentally relate to the material makeup of the "mind" in which it takes place, and that it is fully computational. After AlphaGo, Hassabis and John Jumper developed an AI model called AlphaFold2. The model predicts the biochemical structure of proteins. Proteins control and drive the chemical reactions that form the basis of life. The twenty different amino acids that make up proteins are interconnected into strings that fold up into complex three-dimensional structures.

The bioinformatics scholar Janet Thornton highlights the difference between AlphaFold2 and experimental findings. With AI, you *predict* outcomes. With experiments, you *confirm* them. AlphaFold2's success is that its predictions were confirmed by reality. Biochemistry and biology are good targets for AI, Hassabis claims. They're like "puzzles," he says. AlphaFold2 was able to predict "the structure of virtually all known proteins," according to the Nobel Prize website.

So, is art a game like Go or a structure like the proteins? Can you similarly "predict" all sculpture, graffiti, etching, comics, videos, performance art, music, and poetry using AI? Imagine a force similar to AlphaGo and AlphaFold2, but for art-making. Insofar as something like this already exists, does it succeed? Is art, in other words, a prediction, an experiment, or both?

Human-made art may be associated, rightly or not, with the emergence of "modern" behavior. But it also records many other aspects of lived experience. Think, for example, about *limits* on perception and understanding that exist at any given point in time and space. Think about the material facts of ground truth, like an artwork being unfinished, a storm hitting the artist's house, or a work getting destroyed or lost. Think of the material facts of poverty and sickness. Think of artists who quit making art. Ground truth factors may enforce precarious economies in which the configuration space gets affected—that is, artists will make different kinds of works with different kind of technical means and involving different mental states, but from the same minds.

If you think about art as a game, or a puzzle, you'd probably have to construct many concurrent Go-style boards to model it, each of them exponentially multiplying the number of legal moves. If you think about it as a game, its definition of "winning" differs from how some other puzzles are played and won. If FC Barcelona plays a football match, you don't need a beholder's share to tell the outcome; the scoreboard will say it. With a match of Go, it may be somewhat more complicated to determine a winner, but it is still doable. Yet whenever an artwork wins something, like an award, a jury granting the distinction has essentially been putting their beholder's shares together and (hopefully) has *reasoned* toward their verdict, involving factors other than only the art that was before them. We don't yet have a straightforward model on how to assemble a puzzle for art that can be won like a game of Go. Art is an experiment that emerges from predictive minds and meets other predictive minds in some kind of middle.

Can the unwritten rules be gauged by measuring insane numbers of previous outcomes? If you machine-read millions of computer files of works by one artist, AI could be prompted to predict a next work into being. And another. And another. If you believe that art-making either consciously or unconsciously absorbs its wider surroundings like a sponge, perhaps the longer a time cycle of data capture spans, the more conditions have been *implicitly* taken into account so that governing rules may become apparent that are invisible to artists *as they practice*. It is possible that this revelation is, after all, quite prosaic, and that what gets revealed are an artist's *habits* rather than some deep underlying mechanism. Still, what is the probability distribution that is governing the outer appearances of art? And thus, what is the likelihood that one kind of artwork will emerge rather than another? AI can generate near-infinite predictions that are each as valid as any other, disrupting the quantitative limits that result from material ground truth. By its sheer ability to outpace humans, AI can exceed its own limited existence as a model and impact reality. But it still leaves intact the question: prediction, experiment, or both?

Some artists may be trying to work with AI in a kind of alliance. In order to understand this better, consider the hypothetical scenario that Lee Sedol would play Go *with the help of AI*.

This would not contribute to his status as a human player. It could feel as if he were merely making moves that AI has cooked up. But a human artist's use of AI can, it seems, *add* to their stature. You've got the AI for some kind of foundational augmentation of the output, for some kind of play with the probability distribution. And on the other side you've got the human to make the alliance into a *social fact*—one that can be portrayed on a magazine cover, one that you can have coffee with, one that a collector can fawn over, and so on. You might be asking what the endgame of this is. It isn't even a given that there is one. What gets crafted, it seems, is AI-related art that selects its own internal probability distributions as aesthetic and ideological targets. This might involve quantitative factors—for example, in amounts of output—that sharply differ from what was historically associated with single artists, and might relate more to the ways in which software platforms and the tech industry set conditions for their users.

McKenzie Wark calls the technological mastery of the commodity of information and attention "vectoralism." She terms the "vectoralist class" the social stratum that owns and controls, *in the abstract*, "the infrastructure on which information is routed, whether through time or through space."[7] So is the endgame art *as* vectoralism? In a conversation with fellow makers in the AI branch of contemporary culture, artist and technologist Mat Dryhurst said: "'Well, if you were to look at the last 15 years, who has made the most consequential creative decisions in the world?' You would be hard-pressed to argue that it is people who would traditionally be considered artists."[8] For Dryhurst, these decisions are, it seems, the ones that set *conditions* for a system's outputs. Vectoralist-minded deeper-level rules can have a profound impact on how outputs appear and what they are like. Think not just of the content or meaning of an output—like an image—but also of seemingly innocuous factors like aspect ratio and other system-level decisions. All these rules affect the probability distribution in a fundamental way. Dryhurst—with long-term partner Holly Herndon, whose music always sounds otherworldly, with or without AI—terms the underlying shift in thinking "protocol art." It is a move from looking at specific and particular end points toward a system's decisions in vast quantities of output. Maybe it is comparable—but not reducible—to the implementation of perspective in Renaissance painting. Dryhurst continues,

> Everyone's like, "ok, how do we value a single picture when you can make a million of them?," and that's only going to intensify as the technology becomes more prominent. The way we try to address that problem with the "protocol art" framing is by saying, "Well, actually, the important part is the creation of the system." The constraints of the system that produce infinite media are where the action happens. Who's responsible for the aesthetic regime of Instagram? Is it people using Instagram, or is it the person who shaped the mechanics of the platform who determines that, if you show your face or your leg or whatever, it will get more traction? Like, who's the artist in that scenario? I would argue that it's the person who says, "If you show leg, the algorithm will pick you up." I'd argue that that's an indication of where things are going with these images that AI media generate. The agent that sets the rules or constraints of a system: that's where the art happens.[9]

An artist using AI records the material ground truth of their access to the technology. The algorithm that prefers "leg" will make "art" if it has a bearing on predictions about its perception. Every output needs to pass through a perceiving system again in order to be cognitively appraised and, in a sense, *rise* to being art, or become part of a social circle that values it so. Unless new perceptual relationships are introduced into this game—for example, those between AI models or those with nonhuman perceivers—the dependence of the final output on human perceptual priors might still prevail.

We feel, however, that the *structures designed to capture complexity* can themselves be even more interesting, almost as works of art, than their outputs are. These structures, intensely complex and illegible to direct perception as they may be, reveal how reality is quantified in an abstract configuration space. For example, think about the first photograph of a black hole, produced in 2019 by the Event Horizon Telescope (EHT)—an international collaboration of radio telescopes across the planet. Black holes are "reality-bending" concentrations of matter squeezed into a tiny space, creating an object with an immense gravitational pull. Around a black hole sits a boundary called an event horizon—the surface beyond which nothing can escape the black hole's clutches, not even light. A boundary beyond which almost nothing is detectable for us, preventing us from "seeing" what is beyond it. By multiple telescopes synchronizing and collaboratively calibrating their discrete perceptions, the EHT turned the earth into a kind of camera pointed at the black hole.

With the combined gaze of the EHT, astronomers initially created an image of a black hole called M87*. Later, the joint telescope amassed an image of the Sagittarius A* black hole at the heart of the Milky Way. Sagittarius A* is 26,000 light-years away, or 156 quadrillion miles from Earth. The technique the individual radio telescopes of the EHT used to combine their distinct vantage points into a cohesive image is called very-long-baseline interferometry. To begin perceiving Sagittarius A*, the telescopes picked up radio signals from what circles *around* it. The ring of light that we get to see is made up of photons from the hot, radiating gas that surrounds the black hole.[10]

By using the entire planet as a composite camera, the notion of the individual subjectivity of an artist, photographer—and their first-person point of view—disappears as if it were thrown into a black hole. Indeed, the EHT's being a camera of cameras does away with the troubles of being the single experiencer of an abstraction. To see a black hole you have to let go of your sense of individual subjectivity, or even your ego, so to speak. You can't do Marina Abramović's "The Artist Is Present" inside the black hole. There is no first-person-perspective vantage point left.

Yet once there is the *picture* of a black hole, the question is as banal as *What does it look like?* While a black hole shouldn't look like *anything*—it is understood to be the cliff for information itself—an image of one by the EHT turns out to resemble a blurry half-eaten doughnut on fire. The picture appears to be probing a boundary between measurement and translation, in which the target language of the final result feels like Standard International Photoshop. The telescope itself is, in a sense, more interesting than the kind of picture it produces.

Subsequent visualizations of the spiraling magnetic fields at the edges of Sagittarius A* have begun to look increasingly polished and smooth and simulated, resembling a computer screensaver more than a piece of recorded data.[11] The more these images are drawn away from the actual strangeness and complexity of their collaborative vantage point—the multi-camera, patchy EHT—the more they start to look like 3D-generated models that in turn begin to resemble simulations of black holes that we already had before an actual picture of one entered our visual realm.

Once we perceivers have that famous "photo" of a black hole, it feels a little *too catered* for what our perception already *is*, whereas the EHT's design as a camera of cameras wires us for what our perception might *become*. The photo needs to pass through our sensorial and cognitive biases again. So this links the output of the telescope to a related problem of AI-generated art. By the same token, a system that outputs AI-generated variations of the *Mona Lisa* or versions of Julie Mehretu paintings might make the perceiver aware of an abstract configuration space that informs the probability distribution, but the art still partially takes place in the experiment of perception, in a work's encounter with unknown predictions. So the *systems* that make our perception aware of the configuration space can be more interesting as works of art than their outputs do.

A deeper-level description of art would need to include the dependencies by which art interacts with perceiving systems. Because we cannot directly access the mental states of perceivers to check on their beholder's shares, talk about art often substitutes the more tractable notion of *meaning*. "Meaning," the cognitive scientist Douglas Hofstadter has suggested, "is part of an object to the extent that it acts upon intelligence in a predictable way."[12] It is a somewhat workable proxy—a path through the forest. To attribute meaning to an artwork may, in effect, come down to having a (potentially wrong) working hypothesis about the likely contents of a beholder's share. It's to guess what perceivers are likely to *get*—cognitively and affectively—from the encounter with the artwork. Meaning, according to the linguist Leif Weatherby, is the "unity of reference," not "the signs, words or other contingencies that might be built into natural language and communication more generally."[13] In that sense, talking about meaning is a practical way of compensating for the missing data of everybody's inner experiences.

And there is another possibility: What if in art the latency of its underlying rules has come to be structural? If that were the case, it would make sense to propose that art eventually can't be modeled or predicted along the lines of a puzzle or a game, because its moves—the moves of art—depend on a larger and less easily tractable model of reality.

5

Mirror Neurons

In 1898, Leo Tolstoy published a polemical essay titled *What Is Art?* It had taken him fifteen years to write, and over that period something dramatic had shifted in his life. Tolstoy, who was at that point one of the most celebrated literary figures in Russia, began to turn sharply against the world that had elevated him. He distanced himself from the intelligentsia and also from his own novels. The works that had made him famous had started to feel hollow in the face of the moral torment he was going through. *What Is Art?* was born out of this crisis. It was an act of renunciation, a fire fueled by guilt.

What Is Art? is striking because of what Tolstoy redefines as art. He did not align himself with the established art theories of his day but instead turned toward small, ordinary, almost trivial things: dolls, lullabies, folk songs, peasant crafts. These weren't art objects in the sense that twentieth-century avant-garde movements would later claim urinals or soup cans to be art. Tolstoy's point was different, as he wasn't interested in intellectual irony or provocation. These unpretentious art objects seemed more like cognitive and ethical *prototypes*. In a sense, *What Is Art?* became Tolstoy's farewell to the institutional art world. It was his way of saying that the real thing is elsewhere. Tolstoy recognized, as the writer Arnon Grunberg notes, "that taste is not merely an expression of disinterested complacency but rather an exercise of power."[1]

What Is Art? provides a perspective on the idea that art is not special but instead somehow etched into the everyday of emotional modernity. For Tolstoy, art became a vessel, a medium of communication, of commonality, even commune.[2] Systems like the "art world," to him, obscured this fact.

More than that, Tolstoy came to see art, more or less unwittingly, as a practice of empathy. Empathy might be familiar to you. It's the ability to put yourself in the other's shoes, to feel what someone else feels, and to mentalize about what's going on in someone else's mind. Art was an instrument to do that and transmit the result to somebody else.

The story of *What Is Art?*, then, can't be told in isolation. To understand it fully, we also have to think about empathy in our own time. Because empathy itself—who gets it, how it is valued, what its limits are—is politically and ethically contested. In the following sections, we explore both Tolstoy's argument and the stakes of that argument for us today.

We begin in the twenty-first century. On February 24, 2022, Russia launched its full-scale invasion of Ukraine, a sovereign nation in Eastern Europe that had officially broken away from Moscow three decades earlier with the collapse of the Soviet Union. Back then, Ukraine ceded its nuclear arsenal to Russia under the condition that its territorial integrity would be respected. That promise was codified in the 1994 Budapest Memorandum, with Russia, the US, and the UK all acting as guarantors. Ukraine gave up its ultimate security insurance—nuclear deterrence—in exchange for a written promise that it would never face invasion.

At the time, the idea that Russia would directly attack another country seemed almost unthinkable. The anxiety of the post-Soviet world wasn't so much about Moscow reasserting imperial control as chaos spilling outward from a collapsing empire. Western movies and novels were preoccupied with unsecured warheads, with "loose nukes" making their way into the wrong hands through porous borders. Russia was cast as a broken, lumbering giant, dangerous because of its weakness. The notion that, thirty years later, Russia would reassert itself through outright military conquest—rolling tanks and flying drones across Ukraine's borders—seemed, at the time, the least likely scenario.

Under Vladimir Putin's rule—and really from early on, as he consolidated power and styled himself as Russia's permanent president—a new kind of nationalist nostalgia started taking shape. Nostalgia for the Soviet Union was filtered through an increasingly monarchic and autocratic lens and decorated with religion. So you end up with this strange hybrid: a longing for the Soviet past mixed with an idealization of tsarist grandeur, wrapped up in religious orthodoxy and mired in antagonism toward Russia's many perceived enemies. And all of this unfolded while Russia was also dancing awkwardly through the politics of neoliberal globalization—opening itself to global markets while simultaneously waging two brutal wars in Chechnya.

It was in this cultural and political climate that Harvard scholar Svetlana Boym wrote *The Future of Nostalgia*. In that book, she drew a distinction between two kinds of nostalgia: *reflective* and *restorative*. Reflective nostalgia is more self-aware. It lingers on the ways memory reshapes the past, how the things we feel "homesick" for often never existed in the exact way we imagine them. It recognizes that nostalgia is about invention and imagination as much as it is about memory. We *manufacture* the past we long for. Boym illustrates this beautifully with pop culture references, like "dot.communism," intermixing a nascent global internet culture with glorification of the bygone regime. One of the most striking literary examples she includes is her translation of Giorgio Caproni's short poem "Ritorno" ("The Last Homecoming"), which serves as a parable of reflective nostalgia. The poem describes somebody returning to their home, where they've "never been." Sentimentally inclined truisms like "nothing has changed" turn into a double negation when followed by a dry "from how it was not." There's a glass half-full on a checkered tablecloth that is, all of a sudden, "never filled."[3] So much of nostalgia, Caproni shows, is remembering fictions. The glass on the table has an element of valence: as it is "half-full" it is also prone to be seen as half-empty. It has an energy of its own, dimorphous, letting you best-guess for the state in which you see it first. Even the tablecloth itself isn't a cozy, rustic image of home. The *incerato a quadretti* is waxed, cheap, almost unpleasant to the touch. Reflexive nostalgia, for Boym, is about the messy, contradictory details of memory.

Restorative nostalgia, on the other hand, works as a kind of physically built virtual reality. It is manufactured but doesn't question itself. Instead, it tries to create—almost by brute force—a revamped version of something that can never actually be recovered. It's like chasing a ghost of an "original" that never fully existed in the first place. Politically, that is what played out in Russia. The longing for the Soviet Union got spliced together with heroic visions of the old tsarist empire, and from that fusion emerged the idea of a new Eurasian empire. Meanwhile, the faltering of progressive political projects in the West, and more broadly around the globe, created the conditions for that nostalgia-driven fantasy to harden into an actual political force. What started as propaganda, disinformation, and psychological warfare eventually escalated into open conflict. The invasion of Ukraine in 2022 was the culmination of years of simmering hostilities, stretching back to 2014 with the annexation of Crimea, the covert Russian-backed military operations in the Donbas, and the downing of the Malaysian Airlines flight MH17 by separatists armed with Russian surface-to-air missiles.

That war, and everything leading up to it, forced a reckoning with culture. For Ukraine and its allies, the invasion sparked a deep reconsideration of Russian cultural heritage. In late 2022, Ukrainian culture minister Oleksandr Tkachenko called on the public "to boycott Tchaikovsky until this war is over."[4] On the other side, Russian officials—among them longtime foreign minister Sergei Lavrov—accused the West of "cancelling" Russian art and culture, painting themselves as cultural victims even while waging a war in Ukraine.

Language itself is part of the conflict. Ukrainian was long dismissed by the Russian imperial elite as nothing more than a peasant dialect, unworthy of recognition. Back in 1860, Russian interior minister Pyotr Valuev infamously declared that "a separate Ukrainian language ('Little Russian') has never existed, does not exist, and shall not exist." That logic of erasure has echoed across centuries. Just days before launching the full-scale invasion, Putin infantilized and sexualized Ukraine by calling the country "my beauty," reproducing colonial rhetoric straight out of the nineteenth-century imperial playbook.[5]

So, basically, what we need to get into is the question of whether *What Is Art?* falls within the scope of Russian imperialism or not. And the answer is both yes and no. Tolstoy does use imperial language sometimes. When he describes a hunting ritual of the Mansi people, who live on the eastern side of the Ural mountains, he labels them as "savage." Russia had already conquered western Siberia back in the sixteenth century, and the region became heavily exploited for resources such as gold and rare-earth elements. The Mansi, like other indigenous groups, were kind of "internally exoticized"—made into cultural curiosities while being dominated politically and economically. You can see traces of that mindset bleeding into *What Is Art?*

But then, on the other hand, the text also resists certain pillars of Russian imperial power. Tolstoy explicitly denounces the union of the Russian Orthodox Church with the state, rejecting the state-religion cronyism that has become very visible today.

At the same time, though, he turns around and idealizes the Russian peasantry. He paints them almost as sacral figures: people whose simple emotions haven't been corrupted by the decadent ways of the city. So while he despises the state, he elevates "the people" in a sentimental, romanticized way that is nationalist as well.

What Is Art? critiques empire in some places, but it also reproduces imperialist tropes and hierarchies in others. And that tension—that inability to pin the work down as simply being one thing or the other—is a core reality of Tolstoy's text. So why look at it today?

We are, Tolstoy suggested, surrounded by art miracles of an ordinary kind. In *What Is Art?*, he deliberately privileges things like "an anonymous story about a chicken, the singing of the peasant women on his estate to the banging of scythes, the most sentimental of genre paintings, doorknobs, [and] china dolls" over the canonical works of Dante, Shakespeare, and himself.[6]

What Is Art? appeared to resonate with some broader cultural currents of nineteenth-century Russia, with historical materialism brewing. A popular saying at the time was that "a pair of boots is better than Shakespeare."[7] A similar line, "boots are higher than Pushkin," is attributed to the nihilist writer Dmitri Pisarev.[8] These anti-art, anti-elitist axioms carried an anarchist charge, signaling a revolt not just against art but seemingly against all objects without practical, material value. *What Is Art?* carries some of that same energy, but Tolstoy takes it somewhere else.

His fellow writers at the time rumored that their famous colleague had gone nuts. But the political theorist Isaiah Berlin created a fine diagram for the actual inner conflict. Berlin described Tolstoy as a fox by nature but a hedgehog by aspiration. A hedgehog's life path is dedicated to a single, rock-solid belief. Foxes, on the other hand, "pursue many ends." They are brilliant at improvisation and variety. Hedgehogs are single-minded. They organize their lives around one central vision, one unifying principle. The late Tolstoy desperately wanted to be a hedgehog, and to live by one clear truth alone, but his actual artistic instinct was foxy, sprawling, and multiform.[9] The late Tolstoy, in hedgehog mode, regretted his earlier, foxier ways. He regretted the "vileness" of his youth, and a similar process of reckoning may, at some point, also have informed the denunciation of his own literary achievements.

Some of the remorse focused on the passing of his brother Dmitry. One of five siblings, Dmitry died in 1856 of tuberculosis. A biographer notes that during this time Tolstoy was intoxicated by his own social advancement, "inordinately excited by the life of the metropolis." And when his brother lay dying, Tolstoy found himself unable to summon pity. "He was disgusted by the smell of the sickroom. He felt reproached by the kindness and sheer practical goodness of the women."[10] *What Is Art?* transforms regret about all this into something like a principle. The very qualities that once repulsed Tolstoy become, in his late philosophy, the highest form of art. That's why the book gives so much weight to everyday proto-art objects. Not because they are technically or aesthetically brilliant but instead because they transmit elementary feeling. In this sense, the act of nursing a dying person like Dmitry could be understood as a kind of art, because it transmitted this unpindownable core element. One of *What Is Art?*'s most memorable axioms captures this perfectly: "The good is that which no one can define, but which defines everything else."[11]

It is an idea he had been working on for decades. In *Anna Karenina* (1878) his half-autobiographical character Konstantin Levin voiced almost the same conviction: "If the good has a cause, it is no longer the good; if it has a consequence—a reward—it is also not the good. Therefore the good is outside the chain of causes and effects. And it is precisely this that I know, and that we all know."[12] In *What Is Art?* the good—which appears to exist outside any conventional order of reasoning and problem-solving—is the ultimate objective of every artistic endeavor. Kindness is art. And this is unrelated to what is aesthetically beautiful or pleasing. Tolstoy does not mention that people have done absolute horrors to each other in the name of the good. What he seems to be going for though is the strange phenomenon that is today called *empathy*. It's the capacity to feel, to *mentalize* what somebody else is feeling. To bring about that shared sense is art.

"Art begins," Tolstoy writes, "when one person, with the purpose of communicating to other people a feeling he once experienced, calls it up again within themselves and expresses it by certain external signs."[13] In other words, works of art are externalized proxies to let you feel. They transmit. And this principle gets paired—quite fatally—with Tolstoy's preferred mode of narration: literary naturalism. At its best, realism tries to reproduce the texture of lived experience in detail—the sensory world as it is perceived and felt, along with the inner states that accompany it. If a narrator succeeds, the listeners don't just understand but also feel. Tolstoy writes,

> A boy who once experienced fear, let us say, on encountering a wolf, tells about this encounter and, to call up in others the feeling he experienced, describes himself, his state of mind before the encounter, the surroundings, the forest, his carelessness, and then the look of the wolf, its movements, the distance between the wolf and himself, and so on. All this—if as he tells the story the boy relives the feeling he experienced, infects his listeners, makes them relive all that the narrator lived through—is art.[14]

The premise here seems to be that such a full transfer of inner life is not only possible but also desirable. The boy's wolf story becomes a shift in vantage point, as if we borrow his eyes, his nerves, his pulse. Art is thus a way to create *models* of the viewpoints and, in a sense, of the *minds* of others. Tolstoy extends this logic to other examples, like when he talks about the play he witnessed among the Mansi people. In this performance, a young deer is struck by a hunter's arrow and collapses against its mother. The roles of the fawn, the mother, and the hunter are all played by human actors. And so, as Grunberg recounts, "The audience watches breathlessly, and some even weep."[15] The through line between the wolf story and the deer play is *mentalizing*. Tolstoy seemed to believe that empathy oozed out from the artwork. That the artwork commanded it and that contagion was inevitable if communication was total. Empathy, yes. But the word doesn't feature in the essay. Aside from the question whether he would have wanted it, the concept itself wasn't in use yet.

More recent accounts of empathy place the mechanism in the neurobiological substrate, and not in any artwork. Yet Tolstoy sought an art that would consist only of the condition of being moved, working through the unadorned transmission of feeling. He deployed some unlikely rejected stones of the art world to do so. Hence, the ultra-minimal thingies he favored in *What Is Art?*—crafts, dolls, lullabies, drawings—gesture to the elementary feeling he seemed to want. These aren't "artworks" in the sanctioned sense of the word. They are something like a perceptual kernel—an object almost indistinguishable from the processes it awakens, a prototype for the act of feeling itself. One might call this Art Hedgehog. A version of art that clings only to the objective of moving you.

Then, there is the act of mentalizing. Like with the story of the boy's lupine encounter, the perceiver gets to mentally model and simulate the inner life of another through the channel of art. This is about inferring what others think, feel, or intend.

When we compare these two main threads—Art Hedgehog and mentalizing—they are clearly different. Art Hedgehog is a kind of barren proto-art. It is good only by assumption, its quality postulated, not derived from any kind of reasoning. Try searching online for a homemade doll that doesn't look creepy. Mentalizing, by contrast, is a cognitive operation invoked to understand others' mental states. Let's consider an example. In *I Am a Strange Loop*, Douglas Hofstadter brings his readers to an edge of what it is to mentalize. His partner, Carol Ann Brush Hofstadter, had died suddenly and unexpectedly, leaving Doug and the couple's two young children alone in Italy where they were visiting. Carol's death was not only the end of a shared life but also, as Doug came to realize, the erasure of all moments she had *not yet lived*. What struck him most profoundly was not her disappearance but rather that her *future experiences* had vanished with her. He describes this with painful precision.

> [Carol would no longer have] the chance to watch her children grow up, see their personalities develop, savor their talents, comfort them in their sad times, read them bedtime stories, sing them songs, smile at their childish jokes, paint their rooms, pencil in their heights on their closet walls, teach them to ride a bike, travel with them to other lands, expose them to other languages, get them a pet dog, meet their friends, take them skiing and skating, watch old videos together in our playroom, and on and on. All this future, once so easily taken for granted, Carol had lost in a flash, and I couldn't deal with it.[16]

If this gives you some vibes of American suburbia and a conventional heterosexual family life lived mostly safe from external threats—that's understandable. But Hofstadter's thought experiment in empathy is meant to show the *extent* to which we can mentalize. We can extend it to imagine another's *unlived* experiences in minute detail. And we can understand these experiences as *real*, even if they didn't happen. Doug kind of predicts what failed to happen from Carol's perspective. In one of our film works, *Capture*, we tried to work with the strangeness of this kind of awareness.

The protagonist tries to describe perception and the notion of the internalized mental model. But she signals her acute belief that nonetheless your experiences aren't just metaverse illusions or dispositions:

> Reality, you are saying, does not exist as anything of itself;
> Even if it did, we would not have a way of stepping
> outside ourselves to see it.
> But it is no simulation either
> (for your pain is as real as numbers).
>
> Instead, the world, you are saying,
> like the street we live in
> arises, in part, out of predictions.
> It's a two-way street.[17]

In *I Am a Strange Loop*, Hofstadter jokes about a hypothetical physical phenomenon he calls "feelium." Feelium would bring sensations into being. It would be a missing link between sensation and matter, between qualia and the physical world. Alas, "no one has ever found a single atom or molecule of feelium," Hofstadter quips, throwing cold water on the joke before anyone might run with it. However, "feelium, if it existed, would probably be more like electricity than like atoms or molecules. Or maybe it would be like fire or radioactivity."[18] But point taken. Back to art, the kind of transformation that art produces in us is neither a dose of "feelium" administered from without nor the activation of a hidden reservoir of the stuff within us. Art, as of now, affects the perceiver through the acts of perception and cognition without there being any art particles in play. The perceiver is not acted on but rather *drawn into* a process of modeling. Philosopher Robert Sparrow makes the comparison between ingesting a substance (think "feelium") with exposure to a novel. He argues,

> [It is not] obvious that a pill that renders someone 'more open to the experiences and lives of others' achieves the same results as reading Tolstoy . . . Someone who reads Tolstoy arguably learns *reasons* to be less judgmental and in doing so develops greater understanding; someone who takes a pill has merely *caused* their sentiments to alter. Insofar as moral action requires acting for the right reasons, the person who has learned tolerance from Tolstoy has more and better reasons for action.[19]

Sparrow's point seems clear enough. A poem written centuries ago can move someone alive today. No chemical, no nutrient, no dose of feelium, and—as of now—no brain-computer interface achieves that. Art's frailty—its dependence on mediation, interpretation, continuity, and guesswork—is what also has given it a strange kind of power, teaching perceivers to infer better, toward being moved.

The word "empathy" is a recent arrival in English. It is a latecomer to a fluid idea that has traveled through many languages and moral philosophies. Its lineage reaches back to the Greek *empatheia*, which once meant passion, an intensity of feeling. Over centuries the term gathered shadows; in modern Greek it came to suggest something closer to prejudice or bias. The modern English sense, "feeling into," entered through the German *Einfühlung*. Variants of the idea exist everywhere. In Sanskrit *maitrī* denotes loving-kindness; *karuṇā*, compassion. The Bantu term *ubuntu* gestures toward shared humanity, while the Confucian *ren* names co-humanity. In Māori, *aroha* combines love, pity, and concern into one continuous emotion. Each term outlines slightly different contours of the recognition that self and other are mutually porous.

In the nineteenth century, this intuition began to crystallize further toward the acts of mentalizing. The philosopher Hermann Lotze, writing in 1858, described how the mind projects itself outward—how we imagine ourselves into the forms of other living things. His examples are startling. The mind compresses itself into the "narrow existence" of a shellfish, expands into the canopy of a tree, or even inhabits the mute solidity of a stone. It's interspecies thinking but based on an elementary physical gauge. "No figure is so brittle," he wrote, "into which our imagination cannot lively imagine itself."[20] Robert Vischer would give this projection a name, however: *Einfühlung*. He drew inspiration from Karl Albert Scherner's writings on dreams, in which the sleeping body "objectified" itself into forms and spaces.[21] Vischer built on this to propose a kind of bodily displacement: the idea that we project not just thoughts but also the *shapes* of our own body and soul into other forms. *Einfühlung*, then, was about inhabiting these projections. It was about feeling one's way into a sculpture, a painting, or a landscape.

So empathy, while decisively on its way to science, came to spend a great deal of time in art circles. As imaginative mentalizing, yes, but not yet as interpersonal compassion. So the story goes on. In *Beauty and Ugliness* (1911), the feminist writers Vernon Lee and Clementina Anstruther-Thomson explored how aesthetic experience arises from a perceiver's bodily responses. To look at a painting or sculpture was to *feel* its forms, postures, and rhythms in one's own body. Around the same time, the psychologist Edward Titchener introduced *Einfühlung* into English as "empathy." For Lee and Anstruther-Thomson, empathy was a kind of "moral sympathy."[22] This exceeded mere aesthetic sensitivity, bringing them closer to Tolstoy's views. But not so fast. Lee (the pen name of Violet Paget) had little patience for him. In a review of *What Is Art?*, she accused Tolstoy of lacking historical sense and of being "impervious to any form of science." Locked into a hedgehog's rigid vision, Tolstoy had "become incapable of admitting more than one side to any question, more than one solution to any difficulty, more than one factor in any phenomenon."[23] That will do.

Still, Lee's dismissal revealed actual similarities between their pursuits. Both she and Tolstoy were trying to make sense of a threshold where art crosses into ethics and then further into neurobiology. Both were carving at empathy. And both hit a wall. Lee's conclusion was damning: "My aesthetics will always be those of the gallery and the studio, not of the laboratory," she admitted. "They will be based on observation rather than experiment; and they will remain, for that reason, conjectural and suggestive."[24] The honesty of her words will not be lost on any artist applying to an art-science program today.

While philosophers and aestheticians were tracing the contours of feeling, biology was drawing new maps of the nervous system. In the late nineteenth century, the Spanish biologist and histologist Santiago Ramón y Cajal identified *neurons* as discrete, elongated, tree-like cells that carry electrical signals between the brain and the rest of the body, playing a key role in the workings of perception, sensing, and thought. Cajal's 1904 masterpiece, *The Texture of the Nervous System of Man and the Vertebrates*—also called the *Textura* for short—packaged twenty years of research into a dense double volume, covering 200 different animal species and their neurons.

Cajal's work was equally that of a scientist and an artist. His anatomical drawings of neurons constituted a form of abstract art proper. Cajal rendered what he saw under the microscope into intricate diagrams and networks that were as aesthetically arresting as they were scientifically insightful. With his work, neuroscience as we understand it today was founded. One of his ideas, developed in the *Textura*, was that of brain plasticity: the notion that the brain adapts, grows new connections, and physically responds and changes as it is doing mental work. For Cajal, plasticity was the biological basis of intellectual development. Indeed, he wrote, "the architecture of the sensory centres of the brain, as well as that of the association pathways, is not absolutely fixed . . . The cerebral cortex is a theatre of numerous facts of dynamic action."[25]

Cajal's work also participated in a longer historical lineage of comparisons between organic tissues and woven, knitted, and embroidered garments, using terms such as "thread-like," "knitted tangle," "blanket," and "interlacement" to describe what was found.[26] The seemingly interoperable terms of fabrics and nervous tissues later came to extend to computers, with neuronal structures becoming namesakes for computational networks.

While artificial neural networks used in AI resemble their organic neuronal counterparts only very loosely, the terminology is not entirely random, just as early computing technologies drew inspiration from textile production.[27] The Jacquard loom, with its punch-card system for automated weaving, directly influenced the 1830s design for the Analytical Engine, the first mechanical computer. There's something beautifully transient to the idea of neuronal networks, as there is to their ability to fulfill different functions across the cognitive world, sometimes as a close analogue for computation itself. Cajal's drawings were really like neurobiological diagrams, but they also captured the waviness and strangeness of these structures that mean so much to how we think and feel.

Mental states, thought processes, and perceptual actions have physical substrates, the neuron showed. A major discovery of one such underlying physical reality *for empathy* happened about a century after its discovery. In the early 1990s, researchers studying macaque monkeys found something remarkable. The group discovered that discrete neurons in the brains of a macaque individual "fired" as it grabbed an object. And—here comes the big one—the same neurons "fired" when that individual watched *another* individual grab that object.[28]

The cells causing this were termed *mirror neurons*, and they are regarded as a stepping-stone toward a neurobiological understanding of empathy. Further findings suggested that mirror neurons had a role not just in simulating a perceived motor action but also in predicting the *intention* of that action.[29] There was a *motor* version of *Einfühlung* at work, so it seemed: direct, material resonance at the level of the neuron. Indeed, Tolstoy, in *What Is Art?*, had intuited mirror neurons when he observed that "if a man infects another or others directly by his look or by the sounds he produces at the moment he experiences a feeling, if he makes someone yawn when he himself feels like yawning, or laugh, or cry, when he himself laughs or cries over something, or suffer when he himself suffers, this is not yet art."[30]

The contagion of mirror neurons isn't proto-art. It's really *pre-art*. Just like the pure mirror mechanism doesn't yet explain art, there is further caution about attributing too much causal agency to it. Mirror neurons may be part of a larger system involved with social learning. Thus, "it may not be exclusively or even primarily the individual (mirror) neuron that mirrors others' behavior, but a more complex neural machinery constituted by a variety of cell types that are distributed among multiple brain areas and play an evolutionarily conserved and fundamental role in social learning and behavioral coordination."[31]

Like with art, it appears difficult to track or claim any precise neuronal "site" for the empathy mechanism. Even though mirror neurons are real, empathy, like any complex social phenomenon, seems to be interdependent with many factors other than neurobiological structure. Mirror neurons might explain why we flinch when we see someone stub their toe, but they don't seem to fully explain how we imagine ourselves as a mollusk, for instance. Making that kind of leap requires *theory of mind*—mentalizing. There is, as researchers suggest, "strong evidence that cognitive and affective empathy are distinct psychological processes" that draw on distinct neuronal networks.[32] While empathy is evasive, for us it is still astonishing—in a beautiful way—that it was mapped by science only after art had found it first.

•

Art depends on perception. Until it doesn't. In brain-computer interfaces, where information is given directly to somebody's neuronal architecture, it appears to bypass much of the senses. This would imply a different starting point for what art even is. A work of art becomes the absence of something in the external world. It becomes an internal disposition directly. Some might argue that the experience of art is already neuronal today, so why not bring this reality to its logical end and have art "talk" directly to your brain? It sounds plausible, but how can we prevent that talk from becoming an endless computer-to-brain monologue?

At the same time, it's unlikely that brain-computer interfaces would be made just for art. Art isn't going to become the *only* occupant of such an interface. Possibly you would be talking about art as a *tenant* of a more standardized brain-computer interface. We'd have to talk about the *bandwidth* and the *net neutrality* of a brain-computer interface. Imagine the news, or the art, being fed directly to your brain. Is that really just about getting rid of some external hardware—the device on which you're watching or reading, or the object in the external world? Or might that neuronal shift be ridding you of your very sense of disposition *toward* the information? Is that like taking a sleeping pill instead of reading a novel? And is it possible to still *pay* attention under a brain-computer interface, or is the scarce resource of your perception rather *surrendered* to the product that's wired to your brain? Perhaps, might some mechanisms by which we perceive and empathize at some point get bypassed? In some sense, our ability to mentalize comes down to our capacity to think and feel without separation, just like these elongated neurons tried to tell us, and just like dolls and drawings do too. This is what mentalizing is. And what is its future? The cognitive futures of art might be inexorably bound to empathy.

6

Unknown Others

In the early 1970s the Swedish artist Gerhard Nordström worked on a series of bland-looking landscape paintings. *Eftermiddagssol i hagen* (Afternoon sun in the meadow) seemed to show just what its title said: a pleasantly eventless piece of Swedish countryside. It could have been on Seacrow Island—a fictional place in the Stockholm archipelago that the author Astrid Lindgren had imagined for a lyrical childhood tale just a few years before Nordström's paintings. Indeed, in *Seacrow Island*, eighteen-year-old Malin, after a series of tumultuous events, confides to her diary that "there are many who are crying now and will remember this day with despair." "But for us," Malin continued, speaking of her family, "this day has been so full of joy that I scarcely know how to bear it."[1] Happiness, it seemed, coincided with a close-knit, village-like world. And it was Nordström who opened that world to a larger reality. If you cared to take a closer look, something was clearly off with *Eftermiddagssol i hagen*. Hidden in the grass were bodies. Dead bodies. Victims. Like a cinematographer, Nordström brought in an underhanded but terrible plot. Likewise, in *Stilla vatten* (Still water), the central motif was a quiet forest river, done in a way that might make you fall asleep. But after you looked carefully, you couldn't unsee the dead lying in the river. What was going on?

The paintings were actually about the Vietnam War. Nordström found himself unable to erase images of the 1968 My Lai massacre from his memory, a major war crime committed by the US military on unarmed Vietnamese civilians. The My Lai events happened in the same year that Lindgren's novel was published. The famous antiwar poster *And Babies* from 1969, showing US-murdered Vietnamese children, women, and men at My Lai, can be felt as a direct precursor to Nordström's paintings. But Nordström's take was to hide his acute awareness in unremarkable genre art. Certain people in Sweden are offended by calling it so, but the stealthy approach seems essential. The paintings set up the perceiver for a perfectly nonpolitical art experience. They seemed tailored for people interested in antiques but then delivered something else. We were shown one of Nordström's Vietnam paintings in a messy warehouse space in the outskirts of Lund. The work was virtually hidden between portraits of university provosts, covered with dust from all over the world. Still, it made quite an impression. Nordström situated the victims in Swedish landscapes, not Vietnamese ones. And this implied something beyond mere depiction. It implied, kind of, that the war crimes happened as much in Sweden as they did in Vietnam. They should speak to a perceiver *wherever they are*, negating the cognitive illusion of borders. Subtext: nothing totally separates you from anybody or anything else. Whatever happens to someone else could happen to you. Events are nonlocal. *Suffering is nonlocal.* Nordström reminded audiences of a planetary reality, a single system—"some globe . . . tender as a peach," as the poet Elise Partridge put it in her collection *The If Borderlands*.[2]

This emerging view on the world as a single system began to change what empathy meant. As a social phenomenon, empathy had hitherto been associated with local interactions more than with events happening at a distance. In fact, *art* had been its main medium of displaced reference, effecting feeling for unknown others, like those depicted or described in novels. But mass media changed this. The failure of the US military to keep images of My Lai from global circulation is closely associated with a turn in the public's views on the Vietnam War. As images of wounded and killed civilians and devastated villages began to circulate globally, they inaugurated the path toward American retreat.

That idea—of a system in which what goes around comes around—can be visualized in many ways. One way to look at it is as the planetary circulation of images and information. But it can also be seen as a kind of *supply chain*, in which things we have in our homes turn out to be products of extraction and exploitation in faraway places. The planet itself—through the climate, through its winds and currents—acts as a carrier, bringing information from one corner of the world to another. In Lara Pawson's haunting book *Spent Light*, a protagonist frantically traces how the planet connects all matter and its information—political, ethical, and otherwise—into a red-flag supply chain of tiny particles:

> And there is dust from Gaza in our home. It is in the kitchen, it is on the fridge. I have touched this dust! Have I swallowed it, too? Have I swept it up? Is there dust from Gaza on the broom beside the ironing board under the stairs? The broom that brushes over all the trainers that are piled up and muddled up and waiting to go out and run.[3]

We don't know whether Nordström's paintings played any role in accelerating the end of the Vietnam War. Indirect witnessing—channeled via news images—brought strangers together in solidarity with people they had never met. Indeed, after "empathy" had been introduced into English, it syntactically lay dormant for nearly half a century and only became widely used from the 1940s. As Rébecca Kleinberger notes, "its rise (parallel to the one of the word compassion) accompanies the fall of the word sympathy."[4] During the twentieth century, empathy slowly became a central tenet of culture as it was being tracked across multiple fields at once: in biology, psychology, art, and politics. Scale and a sense of comfort with abstraction and distance may have been important feeders for border-crossing empathy. Socialism, for example, framed itself as an international ideology beyond the confines of the family, the people, and the state. It interconnected separate groups through a shared idea about economic and political realities, insisting on redistributive mechanisms to bring about a more progressive and just society. That insistence, in turn, would have been just an empty prompt without some kind of collective mechanism of empathy underpinning it. Some of the "rational" ideas of the modern age—like universal health care, the eight-hour workday, paid vacation, and other artifacts of social democracy—would have been unthinkable without the tacit belief that the fate of unknown others mirrors your own.

After the Second World War, the Nuremberg trials of 1945 and 1946—where the Allied powers brought Nazi leaders to justice—set a precedent for a yet-unrealized, yet-unfinished system of universal justice. A fragile but persistent notion of, basically, *bearing witness*—however inconsistent and selective it may have turned out to be in practice—emerged as a guiding principle in postwar geopolitics, shaping much of the second half of the twentieth century into its image in one way or another. Again, such an increasingly universal notion of holding to account is also carried by a form of empathy. It is carried by the notion that the suffering of countless unknown others matters—that their experience can be reported and relived, that it can be testified about in a court of law, and that perpetrators can be held to account based on it.

The end of apartheid in South Africa offers an example of empathy's potential in politics. In 1995, Nelson Mandela's government established the Truth and Reconciliation Commission (TRC), chaired by Archbishop Desmond Tutu. Restorative rather than retributive, the TRC created a public commons where victims and offenders of apartheid-era abuses could face one another. As a public investigation whose participants felt with the lived experiences of victims, the TRC ushered in an example of the human capacity for collective redemption through confession and forgiveness. Just three years later, the Rome Statute established the International Criminal Court (ICC) in The Hague. Unlike the TRC, the ICC created a transnational legal framework, enabling its member states to prosecute individuals for genocide, war crimes, crimes against humanity, and aggression. Seen as the culmination of a decades-long process from witnessing to justice, the ICC cast a potentially global judicial net with, yet again, a message that's echoing Gerhard Nordström's Vietnam paintings: *What if it were you?* The spirit of the ICC shaped, to an extent, the ethical vocabulary of liberal-democratic and left-leaning politics as the world entered the twenty-first century.

Media like photojournalism, film, and television made it possible for people to witness—almost in real time—the lives and struggles of faraway others. This in turn changed perception, making it—quite selectively—"global." And while empathy leapt across borders to strangers in distant places, cinema industrialized it, scaling up the human capacity for emotional connection in ways the novel and theater had only hinted at. Video games would go further still. By their immersion in first-person perspectives, having been granted agency in fictional worlds, players no longer simply felt for characters but could inhabit them. We now have a wide range of avenues for empathy to travel: from the social and political identification with faraway others, to bearing witness to, feeling for, and advocating for the victims of violence and war, to the direct pursuit of mirror neurons and "embodied" experiences in simulations, like movies and games.

Yet empathy is no stable force. It operates in tricky and selective ways. If we go back to *Seacrow Island*, Astrid Lindgren suggested that on a perfect day of overwhelming joy and clarity, countless unknown others are crying. Nordström visualized this conundrum directly, but Lindgren hinted at a need to *not* think about it. While empathy has the potential to form a nonlocal model for ethics, at the same time it cannot serve as any sole measure of political, social, or ethical responsibility. So while today atrocities, war crimes, and genocide continue, there is a weird sense that while the evidence is piling up, at the same time people opt out from its perception.

In the early years of the new millennium, the seeming solidity of the Western liberal consensus began to crack. The decade opened with the contested election of George W. Bush in 2000, followed by the shattering spectacle of the Al Qaeda attack on the World Trade Center on September 11, 2001, in which two hijacked airliners struck down America's central icon of global finance, killing nearly 3,000 people. The attacks became the pivot of a new era baptized in fear, vengeance, and security obsession. The US launched its "War on Terror," first in Afghanistan and then, under the banner of fabricated military intelligence, in Iraq. "Sure proof" of weapons of mass destruction was conjured as justification at the United Nations General Assembly. But no such weapons were ever found. What endured instead was a war without end and a bellicose politics of confrontation. Even as Barack Obama, still a senator, warned in 2006 of America's "empathy deficit," another current was swelling. It was a political style dubbed *populism*: a right-wing movement that was at the same time an *affect*, appealing directly to voters' resentment and prejudice, and then a narrowing sense of belonging within an ethnonationalist identity complex. Restorative nostalgia reigned. Its fear and anger proved more sticky at dominating TV and digital news than tiresome explanations by well-meaning liberals could ever counter. Against the backdrop of the first Obama presidential term, the economist and political thinker Jeremy Rifkin published *The Empathic Civilization: The Race to Global Consciousness in a World in Crisis*. The book centered on a catch-22 summarized by philosopher John Gray in a scathing review: "As civilisation has extended the reach of empathy beyond the family and the tribe until it covers all of humankind, the expanding infrastructure of industry and transport has needed ever larger inputs of energy, increasing entropy and wrecking the planet."[5] Centuries of mass industrialization sent Earth's atmosphere into a seemingly endless spiral of ever-increasing CO_2 output. We should act on this entropy through empathy, countering the physics through a common feeling first, Rifkin seemed to argue.

Left in the hands of a self-congratulatory liberal mainstream, empathy became *boring*. It had gone from a wonky philosophy of art all the way to geopolitics in a strange, nonlinear progression. In less than a century it had turned from a "soft skill" to a neurobiologically based competency.[6] But it came out weakened against brute force, its political impact dramatically altered, and liberals have been slow at understanding this. In 2016, psychologist Paul Bloom provoked controversy with a book titled *Against Empathy*. He argued that empathy was not the universally directed virtue it was often assumed to be. Taking climate change as a case study, he asked a seemingly innocuous question: Why do liberals seem to care about it while conservatives do not?[7]

Indeed, how does empathy confront our thinking about those *in the future*? Douglas Hofstadter could envision and think about the futures that his partner Carol would not get to live. And there seems to be no reason why you could not scale that. What about, for example, future generations under climate crisis? Can empathy bridge toward those separated from us by deep time?

Aside from some of some small procedural issues—such as how exactly do you technically reverse the planetary climate feedback loops, how do you capture carbon dioxide from the atmosphere, and how do you form a global political coalition around these policies—caring about climate is socialism for future others. The recipient of the care is doubly distanced from the empath by both space and time. In Paul Bloom's view, doing "nothing" about climate change was the more "empathic" stance, since it avoided disrupting the lives of people whose current jobs and livelihoods depend on the fossil fuel economy. Caring for future victims of climate change, Bloom claimed, was not really empathy but something else, something unnamed and liberal. On the contrary, "it is because of empathy," Bloom wrote, "that citizens of a country can be transfixed by a girl stuck in a well and largely indifferent to climate change." Insisting on the neurobiology of empathy, Bloom appears to picture the public imagining being stuck in the well, taking on the girl's perspective. The psychologist Stephen G. Morris countered Bloom's arguments with research data. Yes, liberals and conservatives do differ in how and for whom they express empathy. But low levels of empathy don't simply demonstrate a preference for immediate conspecifics over unknown others. The connection goes further: low empathy, Morris showed, correlates strongly with climate change denial.[8] It would thus correlate with a significant unwillingness or inability to read or understand abstract data, or events that do not happen to you personally. And while there seems to be a disquieting clarity in Bloom's provocation, his conclusion does not convince. Taken to its logical end, the argument implies that we should only ever care about harm when it touches us—and only us—directly. Why grieve for victims of war across the world if the bombs are not falling on our own families? But the very premise of modern political life is that concern must reach *beyond* the narrow circle of the self, extending to strangers, even to the as-yet-unknown.

The assault on empathy, then, was less an academic exercise than a gift-wrapped thesis for the ascendant far right. In a later blog post, Bloom complained how his work had been taken hostage by far-right Christian evangelists talking about "toxic empathy" and even "the sin of empathy."

So, is empathy doomed to collapse back into ever more

narrow circles of loyalty—family, nation, in-group—so that only the *harm-doing* mechanisms have scaled but not the *feelings* or the *actions* we might take?

It strikes us that low empathy in voters correlates with climate change denial. After all, the denial is not just indifference. It is an active refusal to admit that the crisis exists at all. This refusal cannot really be about not getting some of the basic facts, though these are often deliberately obscured and twisted in biased and manipulative reporting. There is no shortage of data, graphs, and models. There is no shortage of visceral, physical proof. Rather, it seems to come from something more basic: the inability or the unwillingness to see through the abstractions of time and place, and the presence of a phenomenon that's affecting everybody—across these abstractions—yet that cannot be pictured in a single impression. Which isn't so weird, if you think about it. The climate cannot be admired, punished, held, or pitied. In a sense, it cannot even be perceived. For many people, though for some more than for others, the climate seems to happen away from what the senses can actually register. Climate denial may thus partially arise from a hard-wired perceptual and cognitive preference for direct cause and effect. That preference, of course, really *does* tend to misrepresent the deeper reality at a fundamental level.

Consider the spectacle of mixed martial arts (MMA). We spent time watching YouTube clips, and the effect was oddly numbing—frightening but in a boring way. The whole experience is one long rehearsal of motor empathy. Unlike the climate, MMA happens in a cage that limits the perceptual field to a small ring. Gauging, testing, hit follows hit. One goes down bleeding, the other walks victorious. Nothing is ambiguous. Everything gets resolved, sometimes within seconds. It's the dog-eat-dog world of "predatory hegemony," as Stephen M. Walt calls it, rendered in miniature. What remains are mirror neurons firing at the sight of pain and triumph, wiring cause to effect. In the MMA ring, the world is reduced to a single image, a single story: I win, you lose. It also reinforces your instinctive preference to understand a larger world in this way, as a single image that works for you.

There is, admittedly, an enviable focus to such fighting. In its choreography of bodies, MMA even recalls old socialist murals of factory labor—those heroic, grotesque depictions of workers straining at machines. But if, in today's Western information societies, violence has taken the symbolic place once occupied by factory work, this could help explain the cultural mood: the appetite for cruelty, the loathing of nuance, the collapse of empathy. The West, for its part, endlessly compiles lists of others—Chinese, Iranians, Syrians, Yemeni, Palestinians, figures cast as foils to its democratic order. Yet, in mirroring the hostility it claims to resist, the West has become cruel in its own right. Not only is empathy buried, the very practice of understanding—of imagining the inner lives of others—is sacrificed on an altar of "real talk" and tough posturing. Liberalism risks sleepwalking from its dream of universal empathy into a clumsy imitation of the MMA match. One shudders to think what kind of art is already emerging from this geopolitical cartoon. A tough dilemma remains on the terms of this new political sphere, and philosopher Joe Carlsmith captures it with unnerving clarity: "Can goodness compete?"[9]

7
Don't Sacrifice Blue

Art is full of pictures of a sunrise, but it has a much harder time portraying a climate crisis. Claude Monet's 1874 painting *Impression, Sunrise* shows, through a glittering haze, the sun. The work has been said to integrate neurocognitive notions of perception and inference. The neuroscientist Anil Seth has suggested that Impressionist painting, with its articulation of figments of light, shade, and hue, anticipated later discoveries about how the visual system separately processes color and form.[1] Thus, *Impression, Sunrise* would be a case in point of art explicitly addressing intricacies of perception itself. All we see is an orange dot hovering over the horizon. From childhood we accumulate priors for sunrises: lullabies and picture books, classroom sketches, paintings, illustrations, movies, postcards, and, of course, actual sunrises. Kornei Chukovsky's absurdist poem "The Stolen Sun," in which a crocodile eats the sun, preventing it from rising, is an exception that proves the rule: in art, our nearest star is a familiar figure.

As we perceive its ascent through Earth's atmosphere, the sun is throwing billions of photons at us. That energy feels directed, concentrated, nonchaotic. The word "sunrise" is our shortcut, a compression of all this energy into a symbol. Whether Monet paints it or whether another artist does still matters a lot. For example, we love the paintings of the Beirut-born visual artist and poet Etel Adnan, who returned to this same subject—the sun—time and again. Yet throughout all these works, the perceptual principle is the same: all that energetic abundance can be reduced to a single dot or circle, a burning disc we recognize.

For a long time, the kind of top-down reduction that allows us to package "sunrise" has been celebrated as the core of art-making, but that could be about to change. That kind of condensation works when causes and effects can be tethered together—when what we see is what we get. Climate crisis resists this kind of deduction and repackaging into neat symbols and concepts.

In "The Stolen Sun," after the crocodile has eaten the sun, triggering a mini space war, he is forced to spit it out, by which the initial conditions are restored. Had the crocodile been more successful, he might have halted global warming (but have caused many other problems instead).

Earth's fluid domains—the atmosphere, the oceans, and the cryosphere (the frozen parts of Earth)—interact with the lithosphere (Earth's outer surface) to regulate the partitioning of incoming solar radiation. A fraction is reflected back into space, while the majority is absorbed and redistributed in the system. If we look for a core agent of change here, it's carbon dioxide. In 1912, the magazine *Popular Mechanics* warned,

> The furnaces of the world are now burning about 2,000,000,000 tons of coal a year. When this is burned, uniting with oxygen, it adds about 7,000,000,000 tons of carbon dioxide to the atmosphere yearly. This tends to make the air a more effective blanket for the earth and to raise its temperature. The effect may be considerable in a few centuries.

Just a little later, here we are. Unlike the sun, the "blanket" of CO_2 molecules can't be seen. You can't feel it directly. Yet we have deeply enshrined the industrial age, which brought mass CO_2, into our political and social imaginaries. Think of the central icon of the May 1968 French protest movement. It was Atelier Populaire's poster of a factory chimney where, instead of smoke, a fist came out. What progressive political languages might succeed these remnants of the fossil fuel age?

Once released, each CO_2 molecule becomes untraceable, slipping free of origins and borders. This fact corresponds to an insight that the mathematician and theoretical physicist Ludwig Boltzmann developed. A scientist obsessed with statistical mechanics, Boltzmann contended that for any system "there are many more uniform than non-uniform states."[2] Boltzmann's pop status today is focused on the thought experiment of the "Boltzmann brain." He argued that it would be more likely for a complete brain to spontaneously form in the universe than for the entire universe to emerge in the way that cosmologists think it did. This shows the extent to which statistical mechanics for Boltzmann were a field of radical possibility rather than a mere organizing principle for the distribution of matter.

Carbon dioxide molecules spread into a blanket of equilibrium. The odyssey of each individual CO_2 molecule—its *micro-history*, so to speak—could be narrated: its birth in a combustion engine, its diffusion through the air, its tiny role in trapping lots of heat. But if we tried to do that and, say, write a novel about it, the outcome could feel like nothing had happened. While we become aware of the momentous warming that the molecules cause collectively, changing life on earth, at the same time we're lulled to sleep by a seeming lack of plot, of action.

The climate crisis is at once the most momentous story on Earth and one of the least narratable ones. It is a play in which nothing happens while everything changes. Art has long known how to condense energy into powerful symbols. But how does it render the drama of atmospheric carbon dioxide? In his book *The Great Derangement*, Amitav Ghosh meditated on the inability of the literary novel to deal with climate change. For Ghosh, "in a substantially altered world, when sea-level rise has swallowed the Sundarbans and made cities like Kolkata, New York and Bangkok uninhabitable," future readers and museumgoers may look back at the art made during the time of climate crisis and find almost nothing there. Future perceivers of art, Ghosh suggests, will conclude that most forms of art and literature of our period were obscuring the most critical fact of their own time. Indeed, "this era, which so congratulates itself on its self-awareness, will come to be known as the time of the Great Derangement."[3]

Climate change is sometimes described as a sequence of clips of extreme weather disasters you scroll through on social media until one day it is you doing the filming. This description carries a deep truth about perception. That human-made climate change is affecting the planet was scientifically established decades ago and modeled by planetary simulations we have constructed. But you mostly *perceive* that it is real when it is *near you*.

One of art's oldest jobs is displacement. A painting, a sculpture, a poem: all carry reference from one place, time, or mind to another. But on a planetary scale this function collides with a problem: the climate system itself is a vast medium of displaced reference. The information may have already reached us before the art can. The climate itself, as a complex system, is carrying it. A wildfire here is a displaced reference to carbon emissions there. Displaced reference seems *built into* the way climate change happens across the planet through the dislodging of cause and effect.

The irony can sometimes be brutal. In 2021, the IJsselbiënnale, an arts event in the Netherlands, commissioned a flurry of new work themed around climate change. The curators wanted art to speak about rising waters and fragile ecologies as the works were to be placed along a landscape surrounding the IJssel River. Yet before the exhibition could even open, several of the works had to be removed due to imminent flooding. The artworks were overruled by the very conditions they tried to describe, and the flood performed the message with more immediacy.[4] This raises an uncomfortable question: Can art truly "change the way we look at ourselves and our environment," as the IJsselbiënnale promised, when climate change itself is already doing that work at scale—viscerally, devastatingly, and without metaphor, and at the same time without being an object we can touch and feel? It seems that we either have art about climate change that isn't noticed, or we have actions about climate change that aren't necessarily art. This raises the question of what art that is announced as being "about" climate change actually does.

What are ways for art to take these planetary systems seriously as physical entities and carriers of information? One impediment when it comes to storytelling is the very idea of the *story arc*. Most feature films adhere to a three-act structure, a storytelling architecture with near-universal acclaim. Maybe new story typologies will need to underlie tomorrow's art if these works are to be serious attempts at coming to terms with climate crisis. In her aphoristic poetry collection *Shifting the Silence*, Etel Adnan wrote:

> Narration is an outdated form. It's prehistoric. This exercise in futility is close to dying, though it may go on for years. This smoke-screen for anguish takes us nowhere, save to misguided publishers. So we flip-flop toward that core of reality we call silence by talking and writing, illustrating the degree of incoherence our humanity has reached.[5]

One is reminded of the works of the artist Jota Mombaça, who, in the 2022 sculptural installation *GHOST 2: WORDS DON'T GO THERE*, submerged stretches of bleached linen in the San Francisco Bay, by which these textiles absorbed the *contents* of the bay, its chemicals, its pollutants, its noise. The point here seems about capturing a perspective that is narratively arcless. The river becomes a kind of witness, the work of art a kind of sponge.

On October 14, 2022, two women entered London's National Gallery. They went to the room where Vincent van Gogh's painting *Sunflowers* was hung. They waited for a school group to pass, and then it happened. From cans they had concealed under their coats, the pair hurled tomato soup at *Sunflowers*. The Van Gogh was protected by glass, which the soup struck like abstract expressionism. Then the two women, Phoebe Plummer and Anna Holland, glued themselves to the scene, their T-shirts bearing the logo of the climate action group Just Stop Oil.

"What is worth more: art or life?" Phoebe Plummer demanded to know as the soup slid harmlessly down the painting's glass cover.[6] The answer came almost two years later, when a British judge sentenced her to two years in prison for having souped the *Sunflowers*. In the spring of 2023, a profile in *Dazed* magazine of the climate group noted that its actions "subvert the idea of value, and in doing so, draw the public's attention to the government's mishandling of the climate crisis."[7] The piece featured a photo with Plummer as the *Mona Lisa*. Soup can in hand, she wore a Loro Piana garment—an Italian luxury brand favored by the likes of Vladimir Putin (though Loro Piana doesn't love him back, it seems). "STOP OIL" was written under her neck. In the same article, Anna Holland posed as Johannes Vermeer's *Girl with a Pearl Earring*. The 2022 *Sunflowers* action would subsequently be reiterated many times over—for example, with a protester in The Hague gluing his head to the Vermeer. In response, the Mauritshuis, the museum that owns and exhibits *Girl with a Pearl Earring*, issued the statement that "art is defenseless."[8]

The approach was repeated all over Europe. Mashed potatoes splattered Monet's *Les Meules* in Potsdam. Protesters glued themselves to Da Vinci's *The Last Supper*.[9] In Paris at the Musée d'Orsay, a group called Riposte alimentaire pasted a sticker with a dystopian sci-fi landscape over Monet's lovely *Poppy Field*, warning that such visions would be our planetary future if no climate action was taken.[10] By January 2024, even the *Mona Lisa* had been souped at the Louvre, as activists asked: "What is more important? Art or the right to have a healthy and sustainable food system?"[11] This harks back to nineteenth-century calls for dialectical materialism but now with a nod to ecological complexity, showing how views shift from narrow considerations of material security to more system-wide assessments.

To the untrained eye—and to most journalists and politicians—these actions seemed to be solely about creating chaos. In an already hyper-complicated world, activists disrupted what remained of predictable convenience. They were attacking or attaching themselves to tourist magnets and depriving the everyday visitor of a well-deserved dose of timeless serenity—their well-deserved nonpolitical art experience.

As we today contemplate the modes of storytelling, policy, and material action that should befit the climate crisis, it is worth thinking about these protests again. What did they try to expose? Souping *Sunflowers* may have seemed to some to be an attack on beauty. But perhaps the actions' real conversations were with insurance values and financial predictions. A Van Gogh painting is an index of financial value, tourism, heritage, and a civilizational claim to its and its world's *permanence*. We could, by some stretch, call the souping a "design approach." It is a design approach to yet-unresolved questions of awareness, mitigation, and even planetary governance (if such a thing ever could, will, or should exist by our voluntary decisions). It is possible to assess these issues through the prism of a single painting, *Sunflowers*.

We might also see these incidents as an attempt to break a kind of silence that surrounds the climate crisis. But rather than being the art world's 9/11, the souping of Van Gogh's sunflowers added itself to an array of smaller and larger actions where climate protesters try to disrupt the daily routines of art perceivers. Let's consider this disruption a crude form of predictive modeling. All kinds of societal actors—from climate protesters to insurance companies—are *pricing the cost of the climate collapse* into everyday transactions.

Insurance agents and Extinction Rebellion activists currently do a better job of incorporating climate change into their models than art does. Uninsurable waterfront properties are similar to highways blockaded by activists: they translate financially, logistically, what climate change is about to do or already doing. A quantitative portrait is being drawn.

An understanding of the vital role of expectations—and how to change them—occurs in the work of the artist Isaac Julien. His photographic series *True North* (2004) is set in the Arctic. Here, Julien revisits the story of the African American polar explorer Matthew Henson (1866–1955), who accompanied Robert Peary on seven Arctic voyages in the early twentieth century, reaching the North Pole. Yet Henson received little to no credit for his work. He was, essentially, edited out of history. In one of Julien's images in *True North*, actress Vanessa Myrie plays Henson gazing into the Arctic distance. By having Myrie act as Henson, Julien implements a transformation to his character, similar to the one that the Soviet film director Sergei Parajanov achieved when he had the Georgian actress Sofiko Chiaureli play the eighteenth-century Armenian male poet Sayat-Nova in his 1969 cinematic masterpiece *The Color of Pomegranates*. It takes an image like this for us to admit to ourselves that most images repress complexity in lockstep with our perception. Just like the photo of the black hole became a flaming doughnut, it's our top-down inference that does the lockstepping here. Parajanov and Julien make us *deviate* from these priors. But in order to achieve this, they also make reductions of their own. They're focusing on single human protagonists and are ignoring, for example, the billions of people who are not featured in their art.

Sunrises and single-protagonist narratives and three-act story arcs and other well-rehearsed preferences sometimes seem like they're hardwired into our perceptual system. It makes one ask why we should have images at all if these are the underlying standards we fall back to. What's the point? Maybe the climate activists of Riposte alimentaire googled an illustration of a landscape on Mars on the web, or had AI create one, then printed it on a sticker, and then pasted it onto the Monet. So, maybe we *do* have perceptual priors for climate breakdown after all. They're the imaginaries of distant, uninhabitable worlds, imaginaries that were handed down to us through science fiction and airbrush illustrations, with Mars, an iron oxide–cluttered "red planet," coinciding with Cold War–era visions. Are impressions like these accurate pictures of the complex system in question? There are, for instance, no current indications that the earth might be covered with iron oxide because of climate crisis. There are lots of other problems, but not this one yet. Is it important to be precise here? Or are loose metaphors good enough to add to a sense of emergency? We can have pictures of black holes, no problem—but the cameras used to picture them are, in a sense, more interesting than the pictures they take, because they reflect the actual complexity of what is required to get to the image. So, the search to make sense of climate change and art ultimately comes down to a single question: Can we have art about and with complex systems?

In an essay titled "More Is Different," Philip W. Anderson, a Nobel Prize–winning theoretical physicist, argued about the relevance of complexity in the face of physics, a field that was taking on increasing prominence, or even hegemony, among the sciences. Acknowledging the immense contribution of physics to understanding the world, Anderson explained how focusing on *physicalism*—the idea that *everything* is *only physics*—was not just limiting but actually damaging the contributions that are made by other kinds of science. To reduce the world to fundamental physical laws—say, to reduce a painting of a sunset into its constituent fundamental particles—does not imply that we can reverse the procedure and build the painting back up again from these same particles. One cannot explain ponytails or armed conflicts or trade unions or paintings or bird murmurations solely from the underlying physics. Anderson wrote,

> The ability to reduce everything to simple fundamental laws does not imply the ability to start from those laws and reconstruct the universe. In fact, the more the elementary particle physicists tell us about the nature of the fundamental laws, the less relevance they seem to have to the very real problems of the rest of science, much less to those of society.[12]

Instead, each scientific description at a fundamental level leads to a cascade, with the next layer obeying the laws of the previous and with each next layer being less foundational (in the physical sense) than the previous one. Anderson drew a cascade of stacked levels. Each tier obeyed the laws of the one below, but each also developed its own emergent rules. Many-body physics grows out of elementary particle physics; chemistry grows out of many-body physics; molecular biology grows out of chemistry; psychology and the social sciences grow out of biology. This makes complexity real in the sense that the sheer number of concurrent explanations and questions expands along the cascade, and all of them have a bearing on the problems that are complex systems, or the complex systems that are problems.

The intense, lyrically hued skies seen in nineteenth-century paintings by J. M. W. Turner and Caspar David Friedrich are the unwitting sensorial residue of a stratospheric climate event. Following the eruption of a volcano on the island of Sumbawa in Indonesia in 1815, giant clouds of fine particles diffracted sunlight in Europe. The paintings unintentionally became the visual trace of a planetary-scale disaster, demonstrating how our planet is interconnected and singular through ephemeral supply chains of dust. The eruption of Mount Tambora claimed an estimated 71,000 lives in Indonesia and triggered global climate disruptions that persisted for years. It expelled roughly 100 cubic kilometers of ash and sulfur dioxide into the atmosphere, significantly altering weather patterns worldwide. The following year, 1816, came to be known as the "Year Without a Summer," as it was marked by unusually low temperatures and widespread crop failures across Europe and North America. In this way, what appears as a sublime aesthetic in a painting made in one part of the world can be linked to a catastrophe happening in another. To suggest that this phase of Western painting emerged directly from climatic disaster, recording hues and filters of its thinned-out afterlife, would be no exaggeration. So, Mount Tambora's eruption indeed did the opposite of global warming—it significantly cooled the climate for a while. One of the particles responsible for this chilling effect was sulfur dioxide, or SO_2.

Onward from the Just Stop Oil actions lie different forms of large-scale change to turn the tide on the climate crisis. These are variously known as "Green Deals"—mass-scale investments in solar and wind, entwined increasingly with nuclear energy. In the absence of binding (sub-)planetary policies, it's more or less up to each country or group of countries to implement them individually, and each country on its own can claim that it is, when seen in isolation, not significant enough a contributor to planetary greenhouse emissions to implement these costly policies, exposing a structural design flaw to the way in which the nation-state system can—and most importantly, cannot and does not want to—respond to questions that affect a deeper-level version of everybody. Beyond their technocratic solutionism, again, lies the potential for mass movements, such as one based on the larger issue of climate change and ecological and biodiversity destruction. In *Half-Earth Socialism*, Troy Vettese and Drew Pendergrass outline a utopian-utilitarian left-wing ecological movement based on the entomologist E. O. Wilson's thesis of "Half-Earth." The idea entails the degree of rewilding that is necessary to preserve biodiversity and counter habitat loss. Half-Earth comes down to the staggering finding that no less than 50 percent of the planet's surface is needed just to compensate for the impact of human activity. Assuming that market dynamics and government policies will not be voluntarily pursuing its objectives, Vettese and Pendergrass insist that "Half-Earth must be socialist if it is ever to exist."[13] Exactly how you vacate half of the planet for rewilding is a matter of strange design choices: Is it going to be a next-level megastructure drawing a neat dividing line between exploited and rewilded territories? We're thinking of a structure like Neom, the line-like megacity built in Saudi Arabia on political terms quite different from socialism. Or is it (more likely) going to be a hypercomplicated jigsaw puzzle of small Half-Earth pieces here and there, a bit like your daily screen time on your smartphone, which may amount to hours, while it is actually divided into a great many tiny portions and bits? "Some might fault our utopia for lacking a certain grandiosity," they admit. Then,

> Why not build thousands of nuclear reactors or control the climate like a thermostat? Or perhaps master closed systems like Biosphere 2 and then colonize space? We counter that creating Half-Earth and ensuring the good life for billions of people will be difficult enough tasks to occupy us for decades, even centuries. The stars can wait.[14]

The stars can wait, until they can't. While Half-Earth seems in it for the long haul, an obvious third candidate for staving off climate crisis at shorter timescales is geoengineering—the designed intervention with humanmade technology into the climate itself, attempting to rule it more or less with a local or less local craft or device. Given the kinds of event horizons with which governments operate, it isn't too unlikely that this type of planetary "design" (not art) will be found jumping into a capitalist-realist Overton window. The window of opportunity, so to speak. It would require no socialist overhaul, just money and a dose of sheer hubris, every country operating by and for itself alone.

So, geoengineering may halt one crisis, but it could easily usher in another. It would be elementary to expect that in order to achieve some kind of "success," something else would be sacrificed.

In one such scenario, that sacrifice is the color of the sky. This is what's happening in Elizabeth Kolbert's 2021 book *Under a White Sky.* As a consequence of climate geoengineering, the sky loses one of its most defining yet ephemeral figments of experience: blueness. That kind of loss would directly impact art. There's an almost cross-cultural best guess that most skies will be blue, and the artistic tradition carries it. But in Kolbert's future vision, this intangible planetary heritage gets erased. Your perceptual priors will not be the same anymore. So, as Kolbert writes:

> The more particles injected into the stratosphere, the greater the chance of weird side effects. Researchers who looked into using solar geoengineering to offset carbon dioxide levels of five hundred and sixty parts per million—levels that could easily be reached later this century—determined it would change the appearance of the sky. White would become the new blue. The effect, they noted, would cause "the sky over formerly pristine areas to look similar to the sky over urban areas." Another, more felicitous result, they observed, would be glorious sunsets, "similar to those seen after large volcanic eruptions."[15]

Kolbert uses this—essentially aesthetic and somehow painterly—turning point as a critique of geoengineering. The technology, she argues, inserts itself as a new source of entropy into the cycles it is hoping to bend and correct. And there's another problem, essentially to do with the missing political platform to manage and control all of this in combination with the curbing of CO_2 emissions. The institutions that try to platform the necessary governance face massive challenges to their authority and effectiveness.[16] Planetary governance of a de jure kind is nowhere near coming into place. Perhaps as a function of complexity rather than powerlessness, we do have several overlapping systems, such as software and computer networks and financial networks and AI and geoengineering startups that function as de facto planetary designs, but these layers are not yet near the point of rendering climate change actionable and the distribution of burdens *fair*, for that matter.

Re-enter the Mount Tambora scenario. A US-Israeli geoengineering startup named Stardust is announcing its own "proprietary sunlight-scattering particle" that, it predicts, will be wanted by governments soon. The company predicts that "nations will soon pay it more than a billion dollars a year to launch specially equipped aircraft into the stratosphere," carrying the special particles which are to be dropped into the sky.[17] What are they? Nobody knows, because they are proprietary—like a chef's "special sauce." With firms like Stardust doing solar geoengineering, a planetary council becomes even less likely—all you need are paying governments. Particles here, possible side effects (or, *geoengineering slop*) there. If such a solar geoengineering project were to go wrong, it could worsen air pollution and deplete the ozone layer, or trigger major changes in weather patterns—for instance, by disrupting monsoons across densely populated regions of South and East Asia, according to the *Bulletin of the Atomic Scientists*.[18] Stardust's research focuses on "the potential use of sulfur dioxide, because it is known to help reduce global temperatures after volcanic eruptions blast massive amounts of it into the stratospher[e]."[19] Welcome back, SO_2. What the plan comes down to seems like an *engineered* Mount Tambora–type event, without the eruption.

The crucial thing here seems to be that such an intervention by its very character *cannot* benefit everybody. There probably *must* be stuff down the line that you don't want. And the design of bespoke atmospheric events *could* feature that the unwanted consequences affect, let's put it politely, the more precarious and nonpaying ecosystems. *Mount Tambora as a service*. The breakdown of international law and multilateral governance platforms seems a fitting political context for this kind of climate geoengineering. While Stardust's code of conduct mentions that "sunlight reflection deployment should be conducted under established governance, guided by governments and authorized bodies," what guarantees does such a word salad practically give you in an emerging "might makes right" world order? In fact, whose bodies do we speak of? "Do we have the right to do this?" asks the geoengineering thinker Cynthia Scharf, a former member of the UN secretary-general's climate change team. But it could be a case of *damned if you do, damned if you don't*. "Thinking about future generations, do we have the right not to?" she asks.[20]

Climate crisis politicizes causation in complex systems. We seem wired to want our cause and effect in a single image, as a force to an object "that results in a change in its state or location."[21] But that way of looking at things isn't helpful when it comes to complex systems. Complexity arises when "more is different." No single analytical lens can claim to fully understand the system, so perspectives need to work together. Literacy about perception is needed as much as physics and chemistry are, and so are international law and progressive political science. Insofar as art is leading our literacy about perception, it could help us grasp the *more* and the *different* beyond the single image, the first-person perspective, and the story arc. But after thousands of years of art already doing that, at the same time, the climate crisis is its own information system, commanding its own urgencies. While the climate crisis may need to be addressed through rational planning and planetary action—perhaps helped by an increasing intuition for complex systems—the situation equally speaks to our right to sense, our right to feel. The blueness of the sky is a figment of intangible planetary heritage. Exactly how to protect it, how to preserve it, and where, could be a question for climate science and politics as much as it could be one for art.

8

Transitional Objects

We are staring at a JPEG image of a 2,000-year-old chalk figurine. At first glance it resembles something as essential yet formless as a potato. Since it was found near Stonehenge, in a young child's grave, archaeologists guess that it may have been something that the child had played with. The object has short stubs for legs and long ears. It's a pig. Or a hedgehog. There's something about the potato-shaped being that doesn't let the perceiver go. Rudimentary cuteness, maybe. Stronger even, the object is desirable in its very primordiality. In a great way, it is "artlessly unified."[1] Why is it that the world separates out things that are art from things that are cute? It seems self-evident that this object was made by and for humans who were, to quote Sarah Blaffer Hrdy's book *Mothers and Others*, "emotionally modern." With this term, a number of things are implied, including the notion that the social world and its symbolic and material cultures diversify and complexify quickly. So quickly that examples of symbolic externalization, while they may have emerged from a commonly held cognitive root, become divisible into niches like art, language, and toys.

A while ago, we discussed the earliest human-made art with the artist Agnieszka Kurant. She shared with us images of Neolithic basalt pebbles with incised decorations, objects from the Jordan Valley that had inspired her in her own work, which exists on a fine line between art and science. These Neolithic objects dated from the seventh millennium BCE, and Kurant noted that they were likely not just works of art. They were also likely tokens used as currency or for accounting. This ambiguous and multifunctional character seems some kind of benchmark at the cusp of emotional modernity. Moreover, the objects Kurant showed may have been early forms of writing. And they may even have been early *possessions*. Indeed, Kurant said, today we are more or less obliged to see all these forms—art, accounting, writing, money—separated out according to functional differences. But these phenomena may have come into the world more conjoined.[2]

Kurant's words made us think again of the remarkable absence of a dedicated art hub in the human brain or an "art particle" in the physical world. The fact that social, societal, emotional, cognitive, ethical, material, and economic realities *collide* in art contributes to how it, as a phenomenon, keeps escaping precise definition. Maybe art can be identified with an undifferentiated origin story for the diverging branches of the cognitive world. So, along the branches of the evolutionary tree of emotional modernity, *proto-art* may have emerged as some kind of rough cognitive model. (Of course, we can't retrieve the full reality of what may have happened, or how it felt at the time.)

Now, back to what was dubbed "England's oldest toy," the hedgehog or Stone Age Peppa Pig. The object is not, of course, Peppa Pig. It also doesn't have any origins in corporate children's programming. Rather, it is a rough prototype for a companion. Where does she sit in the branches of emotional modernity? She is a potato-shaped avatar to be played with, held, and loved. When psychologists in the twentieth century began to study these objects seriously, some called them "transitional objects." Transitional objects today are soft toys, dolls, comfort blankets, and other external items that young children hold and cuddle and become inseparable from. The chalk pig is not soft, we know, but maybe it was *meant* as soft. This increases its artless power. The nearness of the object to the infant's remains suggests that the two belonged together. Looking at the grave, we see a small cognitive world.

The term "transitional object" was coined in 1953 by the clinical psychoanalyst Donald Winnicott. His partner, Clare Winnicott, a psychologist and social worker, played a significant role in the development of the concept. (When we refer to a "Winnicott" or "the Winnicotts," this includes Clare.) The transitional object was initially thought of as a stand-in for a mother, a baby's first and most essential companion. Moreover, Winnicott imagined the transitional object as a physical bridge occupying the open space that sometimes emerges between mother and child as the child gets older. The transitional object took up that vacant space and provided a continuum. At the same time, the relationship between the child and the transitional object was always dynamic and incomplete. Whether or not the allegory of the maternal surrogate made total sense, for Winnicott, the following things were at stake:

1. The nature of the object
2. The infant's capacity to recognize the object as "not-me"
3. The place of the object—outside, inside, at the border
4. The infant's capacity to create, think up, devise, originate, and produce an object
5. The initiation of an affectionate type of object relationship.[3]

These five points covered the elementary mechanics of the situation. The transitional object isn't the child herself. The object may be closer at hand or further removed from her. There are building blocks of creativity and affect. Basic art-like qualities are already present. They appear to be based on the "not-me" and the need to fill a void, to take up space, and the need to hold. Indeed, from here, a list of "special qualities" of the relationship with the transitional object was formulated. It includes the infant having certain "rights" over the object. This could indicate a possessive relationship but also an unconditional bond, in which the transitional object has voluntarily ceded sovereignty over itself.

Indeed, as Winnicott asserts brilliantly, "the object is affectionately cuddled as well as excitedly loved and mutilated." It seems that the more tortured and inscribed with acts of affection it is, the dearer it becomes. In other words, rather than the transitional object being a kind of brick of gold with intrinsic, essentialist qualities, the transitional object's being *acted on* by a child recursively adds to its value. At the same time, paradoxically, it must never *change*, unless changed by the infant. It must survive instinctual loving and hating. Yet it must seem to the infant to give warmth or to move or to have texture or to do something that seems to show that it has aliveness or reality of its own.[4]

So here's a question that bothers us. Is the transitional object in some way a work of art? And are works of art in some way transitional objects? Children, indeed, may experience their stuffed animal companions as possessing valence and intent, though they are at the same time considered inanimate. Likewise, works of art are not physically alive but rather (sometimes) silent and still. They become imbued with subjectivity—a mental partition that emerges through perceptual and cognitive inference—that seems to make them more active than they are mechanically.

Transitional objects seem to be fundamentally about coping with change, helping a child transfer further into the external world. They are about play, experimentation, protection, affection, mind modeling, recursion, acts of physical love, and maybe, "time and its arrows."[5] The transitional object, as the child's first possession, may be the first thing in her world for which a subjective and dynamic relationship is possible and plausible, a nascent beholder's share. Once a transitional object gets discarded, writes Winnicott, "it is not forgotten and it is not mourned. It loses meaning, and this is because the transitional phenomena have become diffused . . . over the whole cultural field."[6] Similarly, some curators in the art world tend to "move on" from artist to artist, and from artwork to artwork, leaving them devoid of meaning after use. And just like art can look like almost anything, so can a transitional object. The psychoanalyst Dodi Goldman notes how

> having observed a little boy who became thoroughly obsessed with a piece of string at a time of separation from a depressed mother, Winnicott drew conclusions about how string paradoxically both joins and separates. The child's relationship to the string was telling Winnicott something about how potential space both joins and separates the infant and the mother. This is the paradox that I accept and do not attempt to resolve. The baby's separating out the world of objects from the self is achieved only through the absence of a space between the infant and mother, the potential space being filled . . . with illusion, with playing and with symbols.[7]

The child's interest in the piece of string can also be regarded as an act of learning, a first moment of applied curiosity, a first input for a "naïve utility calculus"—or an acquired storage of truths about everyday physics. These factors may, in and of themselves, be as transitional as being temporarily away from the physical proximity of a parent or caretaker. But what is remarkable about the piece of string is its physical minimalism and its non-anthropomorphism.

So, let's do a small thought experiment. Let's try to minimize the physical status of the transitional object. We already scaled down from a doll or soft toy to a piece of string. Now let's go from there to even less. Let's dissolve the string entirely and see what happens next. Even though there is no object, there isn't simply "nothing" left. What occupies that space, be it inner or outer?

•

Some children keep what are called *imaginary companions*. These are figures or personae invented by the child. She is in a relationship of some sort with them, like a friendship or companionship. They are experienced as real, with intent of their own. In spite of this, there is no object in the external world. We might see imaginary companions as *mentalized transitional objects*. Are they in fact versions of the same thing? You can't physically hold an imaginary companion like you hold a teddy bear. The difference between them is sometimes explained by the distinct "character"—a more human-like, complex personality—that children invent for their imaginary companion, exceeding the elementary physical properties of transitional objects.[8]

Let's consider an example to illustrate how any strict distinction between transitional objects and imaginary companions may be challenged. The influential Swiss psychologist Jean Piaget in 1962 documented his daughter Jacqueline's accounts of her imaginary companions. Jacqueline reported "an 'aseau,' a strange birdlike creature that could also be a dog, an insect, or any other animal that struck [her] fancy."[9] Piaget noted how the aseau and other mentalized companions comforted Jacqueline and helped her cope. These are qualities often ascribed to transitional objects. Imaginary objects, indeed, may be seen as variations of transitional objects that require more mental work. They don't have a physical form but still function *as if* they do. They're a bit like playing chess on a purely mentalized chessboard. The physical pieces have gone. Dissolve the chess pieces until only the *fields* matter. That works for frequent chess players who have mentalized the moves, gambits, and positions. It could be similar with imaginary companions.

In another case study, with a child named Lynn, we find more emphasis on the imperceptibility of the imaginary companion (or, in simple terms, the fact that we can't see him). Lynn was asked about how she perceived her imaginary companion, whom she had named Nosey. She admitted that he "was very real to her, but she never actually saw him." Lynn strikingly reported, "I would go to where he was in my mind to see him."[10] Nosey was welcomed by Lynn's family, despite the fact that nobody could see him. Imaginary companions in this way feel related to Andy Clark's idea of perception as a controlled hallucination, and hallucination in turn being an uncontrolled perception. A mentalized object serving transitional functions, the imaginary companion enables a continuity of feeling and contact. Perception, it shows, doesn't always *need* an external thing for it to be nonetheless experienced as real. We can consider this as a path of dematerialization, leaving the object behind and ending up, for better or worse, with nothing else than a beholder's share. Could this work for art as well?

The dematerialization of the artwork was one of the preoccupations of the twentieth century. *Conceptual art*, a postwar genre mainly practiced in Europe and North America, obliterated objecthood, leaving the perceiver to focus on an idea or concept instead. In a sense, the developmental psychology of Winnicott, Piaget, and others formed a partial cognitive mirror for conceptual art, which could do away with the object because it knew, or at least intuited, that the mind is prone to guess forward and fill in more than just the blanks. In spite of dematerializing and dismantling the art object, conceptual art nonetheless left intact some important premises of the art experience.

Conceptual art offered the perceiver a kind of physical emptiness. Some perceivers have found its delicate void to be an epitome of good taste—like an artsy refuge against the vulgarity of visual overload, affirming that our select few likes its art "mind over matter." Much like the way food at Michelin three-star restaurants often comes in microdoses, conceptual art approached nothingness. And that seems interesting again today. Conceptual art's emptiness seems eco-critical with hindsight: without physical works to transport, there was no carbon footprint left to speak of. Conceptual art, environmentally conscious as it now may appear, feels—at its best moments, at least—like a foundational inquiry into the properties of the beholder's share, trying to let go of the idea that this mental partition for art should need an external object at all.

Conceptual art *differed* from transitional objects and imaginary companions because the artists who made it were not kids. They sought the void intentionally and aesthetically. By contrast, a child may be poised to *imagine* something where there is nothing by a force of sheer *cognitive necessity*. Yet the potential of this seeming void as a space giving rise to ideas and information was picked up by the conceptual movement. For example, the artist Robert Barry confided to the critic Lucy Lippard that "*nothing* seems to me the most potent thing in the world."[11]

An example of nothingness in action is Barry's 1969 *Closed Gallery Piece*, in which a sign on a closed door reads that "during the exhibition the gallery will be closed."[12] By art world standards, it is a self-cancelling statement of sorts. Yet, did it yield *interesting* nothingness? It initiated a branch of art that set up new *perceptual contracts* with viewers. Maybe dematerialization proper should be distinguished from dematerialization as aesthetic gameplay. A perceptual contract by which artist and viewer agree to "see" something where there is nothing feels—ethically speaking—less foundational than the perceptual contract by which Lynn's loved ones agreed to see imaginary Nosey. In doing so, they recognized, in some way, *another person*'s need to overcome loneliness and isolation in the social world, playing along with the beholder's share. Barry's *Closed Gallery Piece* was a clever gotcha, showing that categories like *art gallery*, *exhibition*, *visitor*, and even *experience* uphold in the absence of physical art. But construing the riddle of an imaginary companion or transitional object, like kids do, seems somehow based on elemetary needs rather than smart contract-making.

In some works, Barry aimed to direct attention to otherwise unperceived phenomena. His earlier *88mc Carrier Wave (FM)*, from 1968, went further even than the closed gallery. The work consists of radio waves generated by a hand-engineered FM radio transmitter. When amplified through a transistor radio tuned to the specified frequency, the waves produced tones and sounds of varying intensity, depending on the strength of the signal. At the time, "the project challenged longheld assumptions about what defines a work of art and expanded traditional notions of sculpture, positing that sound, as well as objects, can define space."[13] Most interestingly, *88mc Carrier Wave* is an intentional series of signals that can be found somewhere ephemeral, on a radio frequency, almost by chance. It could easily be missed or overlooked. Indeed, conceptual art, at its most interesting moments, seemed to attempt to reach out to the limits of commensurability, opting for a fragile existence on the edge of the noise of being. And it minimized, like the imaginary companion, the difference between a work of art in the world and one that is perceived by the mind alone.

We have been looking for an elementary typology for art, one by which it is not "special" and perhaps not even always that artful. Art is not some kind of ornamental add-on to the ordinary sludge of existence. Instead, we surmise, it emerges with processes at the heart of cognitive, social, and emotional life. If anything, *these* processes are the ones to be called special. Relieving art from some of its elevated status would make it more widespread and at the same time less noticeable than it had been before. Maybe the transitional object can be seen as a typology for aspects of art that tend to dissolve with the branching out of objects and practices into the wider cultural field, like a bit of a catchall for affect, objects, and imagining.

And though aesthetics are often considered to belong with art, our arguments so far have had little to do with them. We have purposely avoided talking about the aesthetics of the potato-shaped primordial hedgehog toy. Inquiries about its beauty, or lack thereof, would miss the point. Separating the transitional object out from art *in general* was the initial category mistake. That *beauty* became optimized in *some* art should perhaps be considered further specialization rather than an elementary quality. So, in short, we have been looking at art as something foundational and necessary to the cognitive and social world.

Transitional art would enable ordinary people to cope with or express something about things like change, joy, departure, and death. To both cope with and initiate the flux of change and the blurring of fixed categories. This art relates to coping with distance; it relates to filling the void that's left behind, a void that all of us confront, which is as much to do with space as it is with time.

And though it was not explicitly sought out by Winnicott, cuteness seems to be part of it too.What is cuteness? The way of the cute seems, in one part, to appeal to our inclination to hold something dear. Indeed, as Sianne Ngai suggests, "cuteness solicits a regard of the commodity as an anthropomorphic being less powerful than the aesthetic subject, appealing specifically to us for protection and care."[14] Ngai seems to be handing us a cipher for the split between art and transitional objects. We saw that split happening earlier, with the Stone Age toy hedgehog. Through the cute, Ngai appears to suggest, an object's aesthetics become less powerful, allowing for the impulse to care. This dynamic heterarchy of priorities has the potential to unify aesthetics with aspects of life that often remain on the verge of art, like acknowledged dependence, first encoded in the child but in fact encoded in everybody throughout life.

Alice Dos Reis submits that there is a "'cuddly nearness' about cuteness that seems to both upset and disenchant traditional patriarchal modernist ideals about the aesthetic 'sublime.'" Crucially, she writes, "cuteness is considered too much of something that is too little, hence discarded as an as aesthetics of otherness."[15] From there, we could talk about cuteness being unleashed into culture. This is where, perhaps, something more is at stake than the appeal for care. The appeal to vulnerability is not the whole story of cuteness. Cuteness would not be as interesting as it is, were it not *also* ambiguous, mischievous, witty, and even a little monstrous. A more complex, ambiguous, or dimorphous aspect belongs with it, a resistance to categorization and binaries. To enact a reversal of the splitting of the world into the self-proclaimed important and the seemingly insignificant, a monstrous kind of cuteness is needed.

In the famous Japanese anime film *My Neighbor Totoro* (1988) by Hayao Miyazaki and Studio Ghibli, a cast of forest spirits represents both danger and joy, blossoming nature and supernatural abyss to the film's child protagonists, Satsuki and Mei. Totoro, the evasive being at the heart of the forest, is lovable but appears to be dangerous too. A superlative of ambiguous cuteness is an eerily grinning twelve-legged chimera of furry-tailed cat and bus called Nekobasu (Catbus). "It" drives and then flies Mei and Satsuki to their hospitalized mother (like a transitional object in the world of the Winnicotts, a bridge between parent and child). Catbus emanates something illegible, opaque, otherworldly, potentially dangerous—but transitional. And cute. Catbus seems to foreshadow what the philosopher Simon May has referred to as the "power of cute." The power of cute takes us beyond its appeal for protection and care, imbuing it with a force to be reckoned with. In line with the powers of transitional art, May wades into ambiguity and indeterminacy as hallmarks of the power of cute. Cuteness, he suggests, is "a teasing expression of the unclarity, the uncertainty, the uncanniness, the continuous flux or 'becoming' that our era detects at the heart of all existence, living and nonliving."[16]

Everything is becoming. A final state will never be reached. So the blurring of categorial boundaries that signifies May's "era of cute" begins with a meltdown of the adult-child distinction.[17] It proceeds to the meltdown of the binary gender distinction. But the blurring of age itself could be seen as resistance against linear time and linear progress as well. In the very sense of the arrow of time being, in our macroscopic understanding of it, irrevocably pointed toward the future, an inversion of prominence between adult and child could be interpreted as a revolt against time itself moving forward, with that arrow being sent in reverse.

A parallel track about transitional objects involves the phenomenon of the *daemon*. Indeed, "the history of thought regarding human creativity comes pre-laden with such mysterious concepts," writes Ana-Maria Olteţeanu.[18] "Daemon" originates from the Greek *daimōn*, a lesser deity or guiding spirit.

By way of an extended take on Winnicott's transitional boject, daemons feature prominently in *His Dark Materials*, a series of sci-fi/fantasy novels by the author Philip Pullman. Though movies were made of them, our references will be to only the books. Not unlike the work of Ursula K. Le Guin, their writing resists pre-visualization by a third party. It *wants* to be visualized by a reader.

In this exhilarating epic, inspired by physics, philosophy, and theology, humans have lifelong companions called daemons. A daemon is an outward manifestation of a person's character as it is known or perhaps unknown to them, embodied in the form of an animal. It's like an externalized soul worn on the sleeve. A human and their daemon have to be together always. A child's daemon may change from moment to moment. For example, protagonist Lyra Belacqua's daemon, Pantalaimon, or just Pan, is often a moth but can also transform into a wildcat or a gull or an ermine or a mouse, and Lyra has no control over the metamorphosis. The oftentimes apparently inexplicable shapeshifting fits with what Karen Gallas, a schoolteacher-researcher and author, has identified as "the serious work that children do below the surface."[19] The daemon, it seems, is the externalization of that work, giving it a tangible, living shape. Thus, shapeshifting, ongoing transformation, like in Gallas's collection of essays *Sometimes I Can Be Anything,* is not superficial. It reflects emotions and preoccupations at a deeper level. Locked into mutualism, Pan can be a voice of reason in Lyra's troubled moments. But when transformed into a seagull, Pan skirts the waves jubilant, carefree. Then, suddenly, at a certain age, a daemon's animal shape becomes permanent.

As it fixes into a final shape, the daemon here somehow ceases to be fully transitional. Though it's still an animal-shaped companion fully interdependent with its human other, the daemon seems to have evolved into something much more predictable here. It has shed the child's serious work under the surface. It has become a bit more like a person's singular outward "icon" or "symbol"—a kind of statuette in motion, a proxy for a personality that itself has gotten hardened in its ways. Maybe, it has become top-down (concept-first) instead of bottom-up (sensing-first).

Yet, transitional objects—plush agents of coping—are about *not-hardening.* They remain transient through categories, lapidary definitions, and ossified predictions. The transitional object bridges binaries, boundaries, causes, and distances: female-male, child-adult, past-future, alone-together. They are sensing-first. When seen in this way, the transitional object is about what remains new and unfinished in familiarity.

Transition—or queerness—can touch subjects as traditionally overdefined as classical musical instruments and their virtuoso players. This becomes perceptible in the work of the composer inti figgis-vizueta. In her *Music for Transitions* (2020), a piece for solo string and fixed media written for and performed by cellist Andrew Yee, figgis-vizueta connects patterns that may once have been named *serial* but are better called *emergent*. The difference between both seems to be about the nature of repetition. Many of figgis-vizueta's compositions invoke the sensation of bird murmurations. It happens in *Music for Transitions* by a subsequent overlay of cello voices by Yee. "Transitional" qualities emerge when the patterns evolve to become more than the sum of their parts. In an eponymous concert in 2023—an "unbroken dialogue" with works by figgis-vizueta, Yee, Caroline Shaw, Nico Muhly, and Leilehua Lanzilotti—the compositional techniques in use were analyzed by composer and violinist Chrysanthe Tan as "rooted in sensory experiences ... When a child picks up a violin for the first time, they don't play scales and arpeggios; they slide and wiggle their fingers around, make unpredictable noises, and occasionally discover things that vibrate in pleasing ways."

This brings us back to the transitional object's agency between definitions. It belongs with longing, with being longed for—with loving, and being loved—as processes instead of final states. In its classical definition, a daemon was an inner voice of advice coming from a deity caught between two worlds. In an exposé about "analogical aliens," Claire Webb writes,

> Socrates . . . learned the true nature of love, he revealed, after having been chastened by a wise woman, Diotima. We learn that from his mother, Poverty, Eros is "always impoverished . . . always in need," but from his father, Resource, is at the same time "a schemer for beautiful and good things." Diotima tells Socrates that Eros is "neither immortal nor mortal," but instead, a "daemon" caught between those realms, always reaching for the divine. The wise woman specifies that Love is not statically contained in a vessel of the beloved, but a dynamic "lov*ing*," a performance that strives toward the divine.[20]

This short passage feels related to what is interactive, recursive, and process-oriented about a transitional object, and the continuous acts of loving that make it real for a child. And also to what distinguishes such a dynamically shaped relationship from one with a merely valuable or rare object. At some point, any analysis of either transitional objects or art must confront what psychologists have called *essentialism*. Essentialism is said to entail our intuitive beliefs about the true character of things.

Let's put it like this: an original (and, inevitably, visually striking) Julie Mehretu painting and an intensely cuddled and shredded teddy bear might share no aesthetics with each other to speak of. Yet, as original objects, they are both completely irreplaceable to their respective owners, or makers, in the sense that Mehretu is the maker of her painting and a child is, in fact, the maker of their transitional object, whether or not they have physically manufactured it, in whole or in part. Note that irreplaceability might have different implications for owners and makers. In the case of Mehretu, the owner may often be somebody else. In the case of a transitional object, owner and maker coincide. It is a bit tricky, as the question becomes what encodes that irreplaceability, or where it gets encoded.

For the psychologist Susan Gelman, in her 2003 book *The Essential Child*, essentialism was "the view that categories have an underlying reality or true nature that one cannot observe directly but that gives an object its identity."[21] Essentialism is said to govern feelings that people, especially kids, have about the authenticity of things. It sits quite uncomfortably with the ambiguous qualities of the transitional object, and it could just as easily be interpreted as a free ticket for people to affirm their biases. The problem seems to have been reckoned with in Gelman's own later redefinition. By 2013, she had updated her description, now calling essentialism a "folk belief."[22]

•

Our own field research about essentialism and the doll includes an exchange of questions with our child, then aged eight. On their request, we're using the name X here—bearing no reference to the infamous social media platform. We were traveling through Italy between two pandemic lockdowns. X was always accompanied by a plush red panda, Amy. We asked them what would be the difference between Amy and an exact replica. Similar hypotheticals have been introduced in psychological experiments around essentialism, in which the objective seems to have been to verify the presumption of an unchangeable inner core in an object or person.

X had two arguments for preferring the real Amy to a new one brought in from the store. One was that "the real Amy has been hugged by me" (while the replica had not). The other was that "the real Amy had already become part of stories" (while the replica had not).[23] X's arguments had nothing to do with the essentialist line of an inner secret nature. They seem to be about properties added by a child's imaginative play, in tune with hugging-as-inscribing. They seem more consistent with Winnicott's regard for experiment and in tune with what Diotima told Socrates about loving. Maybe X's account also relates to what the author N. Katherine Hayles calls "continuous reciprocal causation," citing, in turn, the cognitive scientist Andy Clark.[24] Reciprocal causation means that *things cause each other.* Instead of there being a static, linear process with a singular cause toward an essentialist, worshipped vessel of the beloved, there's more of a feedback loop going on, in which the transitional object is imagined to reciprocate its becoming part of their cognitive world. And so on. By imagining, participating in stories, and being hugged, reciprocity becomes real. Essentialism, it seems, overlooked how children are not merely owners of transitional objects but also their makers. They are the ones who bring these objects to life, not unlike what artists do with their works.

According to Dos Reis, "cute" (or, thus, transitional) objects were barred from access to *art world* aesthetics for largely patriarchal reasons. If the transitional object is a half-baked daemon, it is a way station for the child, associated with her yet-undeveloped powers. Indeed, in the work of the author bell hooks, the daemon is linked to the talent for making art. "Within our all-black churches," she writes, "we were taught to value talent, what old folks called 'the gift.' " In these stories, hooks writes in *Art on My Mind*, "we were taught that no matter the circumstance, class, gender, or race, if the divine spirit had given one the 'gift'—the capacity to create art—then one had to yield, to surrender to that calling."[25]

Another jab at the transitional object was featured in the artist Mike Kelley's *Ahh ... Youth!*, in which he accumulated homemade dolls bought from thrift stores and portrayed them in series of photographs and sculptures. The work is described in ways that bear a striking similarity to postwar US developmental psychology. Indeed, whereas Selma H. Fraiberg, a contemporary of Winnicott, had referred to early childhood as a "submerged city," in Kelley's work, in the words of the Metropolitan Museum of Art, "these soiled and ratty objects—cherished and then discarded—were like totems from the lost continent of childhood that, while often barely remembered, shape and determine our adult selves." The submerged city and the lost continent might both refer—as metaphors—to a foundational but barely remembered early childhood. And, the description continues, "stitched into caftan-like wall hangings or posed in combinations on children's blankets, Kelley's stuffed animal works struck an explosive chord in a culture of protracted adolescence ... dark, funny, and sad works about memory and loss."[26] One of the portraits became the sleeve art for Sonic Youth's album *Dirty* (1992). Given the historical context, should we consider these rag dolls now *postmodern*—that is, made part of what Fredric Jameson has called "the cultural logic of late capitalism"? The latter seems to be the case if we consider what Kelley had to say about them, homing in on the labor of love that their makers spent, and the transactional value they represented as unrepayable tokens. As Kelley noted,

> The first piece I did with stuffed animals ... wasn't even about stuffed animals but was about gifts. That was because the primary discussion in the art world at that time had to do with commodification. There were these Utopian ideas being bandied about, "Well, we can make an art object that can't be commodified." What's that? That's a gift. If I give you this art-thing, it's going to escape the evils of capitalism.[27]

Kelley's witty take only affirms how paid and unpaid labor, art and gift, have ended up at radically different places in emotional modernity. Even if it does point back at a broadly shared ancestry, the transitional object occupies a different branch from most art today. The transitional object is an unconditional commitment outside of the sphere of economic exchange.

Amy, the plush red panda, was lost somewhere in or around the village of Radda in Chianti, in rural Tuscany, near Siena, during the summer of 2021. When something of value gets lost like that, it's like a kind of Bayesian lightning strike. Your previous impression of the world had things in order. When something dearly loved disappears just like that—into the abyss of an enormous, chaotic background—it makes you instantly see how many variables you'd been taking for granted. In even the simplest of everyday realities, we unsee most things. Now Amy is gone. Distressed, we try to roll back time and memory to the moment just before it happened. We try to fold back entropy. We try to fold reality back to its prior, less-dispersed state, when Amy was still here. Expeditions to find her—crisscrossing through the sun-swept hills, scouring derelict parking lots with insular picnic tables for traces of an intensely loved red panda—came to no avail. Entropy is about what gets more dispersed, and now this included Amy, who fell into the noise. It touches, again, on the problem of empathy. Almost nothing disperses by its own choice. Maybe this is the *emotional texture* of entropy and why the transitional object forbids it. We experience time and its passing as we see smoke billowing from chimneys, never to return. Eggs breaking never to be unbroken, vases shattering not to return to their original, wholesome shapes. We narrate the loss of self-containment. We disperse the ashes.

Maybe, then, this is something we learn at a young age about how the world works. In physics, entropy signifies a kind of *temporal asymmetry*: things on the timeline, or in the time series, look different in the beginning than later on. They don't mirror each other at all. In some way, the transitional object counters this, arguing for a past and a future that look reassuringly similar. Maybe entropy, and what we learn about it from the world around us, says something about why a first "not-me possession" really needs to be *permanent* and *always available*. The transitional object already was studied as a spatial bridge. But it could be a *temporal* bridge all the same. Maybe the transitional object is something like a child's first defense against the arrow of time.

Back from Tuscany, a first pass at a replacement panda, brought in shortly after Amy was found to be missing, was unsuccessful. X tolerated it but didn't cognitively embrace it. Yet, after some time, another panda made the cut. Red, as X named it immediately, became as close to them as Amy had ever been.

Having now become thoroughly fascinated by the transitional object, we hoped to feature Red in our next film, which was going to be an adaptation of a series of poems by Eugene Ostashevsky. *The Feeling Sonnets*, first published in 2022, collects Ostashevsky's verse around feeling, language, and being lost and found in translation. For the script of *The Feeling Sonnets (Transitional Object)* we wrote a small monologue for a fictional scientist trying to explain the transitional object along the arrow of time:

> Any child will cling to their plush animal. As a means of time travel. As a way of staying in touch with the ungraspable nature of time. The child is attempting to restore temporal symmetry, in which past and future have the exact same shape. And can be travelled in both directions, forward and backward. The transitional object is not merely a replacement for the absent mother, but a means to give agency and grounding to actions taken in the absence of parents in general. The plush animal is a way to travel through time, and thus, through space. Plush animals, once lost, are irreplaceable by identical copies brought in as consolation. The transitional object is temporally symmetrical.[28]

Another experiment with the transitional object involved palindromes. Palindromes are words, phrases, or sequences that read the same backward as forward. For example, "mom" is a palindrome. So are "pop," "noon," and "evil olive." In both directions you get the same information. This makes them not just visually but also *temporally* symmetrical. When we prompted ChatGPT to write palindromes based on an input sentence from Ostashevsky's *The Feeling Sonnets*—"Feelings fork like the capillaries of a leaf in the forest"—we found that, while the chatbot could define palindromes, it could not necessarily create them. This was 2023. It generated outputs like "Able I trace car ice art Elba," "Red roses run no risk sir order," and "Too hot was I," all somewhat cute, but also somewhat (or very) incorrect. The broken symmetry in these ChatGPT-generated outputs may have been due to the size or granularity of the tokens (the units of text in the underlying model, out of which it rebuilds language). If you think of the tokens as building blocks for larger sequences of meaning, they also will need to be the same in both directions. Likewise, broken symmetry in these generated outputs may have been caused by the limits of next-token prediction—as a palindrome asks you to predict from the end of a sequence in reverse, just as you predict forward, and meet in the middle. Predicting forward and in reverse, arriving at a valid sequence.

We see the river run by our house. Although we don't know what it even is, we experience that time "passes." The philosopher of physics David Albert has found a fitting name for what we deduce from this. He has called it the *Past-Hypothesis*. The working hypothesis comes into being with our colloquial experience of entropy. None of this will be seen to return anytime soon to its more self-contained prior state.

Art is a bit timeless, like pricelessness. Yet the original bond between the child and the transitional object seems much like a bond with art. Amy and Red may never fall apart. Both art and transitional objects hold what cannot be, should not be, categorized. Is art a transitional object?

9

Topsy-Turvies

D: We wanna get on about language because we started with *poetry* when we became parents. That fascination with poetry was about the babbling of a child. The first word our child said was

V: Book.

D: My dad was literally on his deathbed when he gave her a book full of absurdist rhymes. In the thick of the fog of mourning his passing, we read the children's poetry he'd given her. So, we read of things that cannot be in reality. Topsy-turvies, upside-down worlds. Everything is one thing and its opposite at the same time. Which seemed the only kind of statement that made sense at that moment. Laughing through tears.

V: Children have the gift of fantasy *and* of telling the truth. They are topsy-turvy by nature.

D: What do you actually want to spend time with? Technology or children? When you get to choose between technology and children, the choice is easy, right?

V: Technology. Or what's left of it. Or what it's become.

D: Children.

V: Can we give an example of absurdism by children?

D: *In January, on the fifth of April,*
In dry weather—with knee-high puddles.
On a brick street—made of wooden planks
Walked a tall man—of short height.[1]
Why do young children tend to find this funny?

V: Because they take language to be a medium with which

we say things that are true. And these are things that can't be true at the same time. And that's funny.

D: Yeah. That's mischievous. Which one of the three possibilities is the case? One, or two, or neither? What we are asked to picture counters our intuition completely. You can't both be in January and on the fifth of April, right? Catch me if you can. I, *actual fact*, am elusive. But now let's speed things up. If you accelerate this kind of absurdism this is what you end up with:

John Stewart Bell
Speakable and Unspeakable in Quantum Mechanics
Cambridge University Press, 1987.

V: Let's talk about that later.

•

Parenthood is the responsibility that befalls a child's primary caretakers. While biological parents share traits with their children, the subjective gaze of parenthood—the sense of *what it is like* to be a parent—doesn't depend on a biological architecture alone. Being a parent, then, isn't primarily about being bonded by genetic linkage; it is about working at being unconditional. Parenthood is a strange loop about the recursive sensation of carrying and being carried at the same time. After the passing of her mother, the writer Clarice Lispector (1920–1977)—whose novels explore visceral, proto-conscious interactions and bodily states—said that, if it weren't for being a mother, "I would be alone in the world."[2]

Art changes because of the contributions that children make to it as its creators, perceivers, and commentators. Indeed, as the teacher-researcher Karen Gallas comments, while we "relegate the adaptive use of song, movement, painting, sculpting, drama, and poetry to a small segment of our population, [this does] not confirm that those areas of expression are only available to a few."[3] In other words, specialized discussion of professionally produced art happens with the unspoken premise that art has a more general presence in life. The philosopher, theologian, political activist, politician, and social critic Cornel West says with typical passion, "The music that you heard, the poetry that soaked your soul, it is in no way ornamental. It is in no way decorative. It ought to be constitutive of who you are."[4]

With children at its source, the cognitive river of art can seem full of unexpected clarity. For example, X, our child, after having watched our film *Capture*, called their close friend A on Signal and relayed that "it is fiction but it is not a story!" (This is a very fitting comment if you happen to know the kind of films we make.) The poet Anne Boyer, in a striking essay on breast cancer, notes how her daughter suggested to her to invent "a symbol for my writing that marks an interruption in it." These kinds of interventions by children are forms of poetry in and of itself, especially as they appear entirely unscripted. Boyer, at the end of her essay, adds that "what is hidden in the moment that interrupts poetry" is, indeed, "poetry."[5]

In this chapter we will be discussing absurdist poetry and the appeals that it makes to children's and adults' intuitive understandings of the way the world works (or is said to work). "Absurdism" is itself a flawed term for works ranging from topsy-turvies (verse made out of self-contradictory statements) to surrealist fables (think, for example, of Leonora Carrington's short story "White Rabbits," situated at a "40 Pest Street" in London) to sound-based poetry that interrupts the communicative function of language itself. What these poetic utterances have in common is that they steer the listener toward cognitive play. They seem in agreement with Boyer, who told *El País* in 2024, "I don't believe that beauty heals. I believe in an art that helps you think."[6]

•

If you listen to a child's first speech acts, you may find that they do not consist of words but rather of *sounds*. We measure the result that these sounds produce by something other than their effectiveness at transacting. *Babbling* is a linguistic primordial soup among children across species. In human children, new words stumble from this soup. Some of them are nonsensical. They *are* the soup. Language acquisition involves imitation, but also imagination. It's a computational soup. Computational linguist Gašper Beguš puts the two together and calls the result, quite wonderfully: *imagitation*. "Imagitation" as a word is also the product of the process that it describes. It's invented, concatenated from two others. "Imagitated" expressions offer glimpses of a *latent space*: an unobserved space of language in formation, a series of interior snapshots of language in its stage of becoming. Beguš's concept of imagitation emerges from his study of generative adversarial networks, or GANs. These artificial neural networks output language through iterative imitation of a very small set of input items—for example, audio data of only a few spoken English words. The GANs are thought to somewhat match the way human babies learn to talk through their output of "innovative lexical items that violate training data, but are linguistically interpretable and highly informative for cognitive modeling"—a kind of computational babbling. The notion of being "informative," then, seems to point at exceeding the training data, thereby making the result a bit harder to compress and predict in comparison to the material that the system was trained on. Indeed, a "network trained on *suit* and *dark* outputs [the] innovative *start*, even though it never saw *start* or even a 'st' sequence in the training data." This kind of result, for Beguš, can be "directly paralleled to productivity in human speech."[7]

In his book *From Two to Five*, the translator, editor, critic, poet, and writer Kornei Chukovsky (1882–1969) wrote about "verbal cuteness," and it pointed at something quite like imagitation. For example, a five-year-old child named Ira inferred that her grandfather's brain might contain "straw." Why? He doesn't seem to be very "decisioned," she said, concatenating "decision" and "decided." "Decisioned," then, is about halfway communication. It needs guesswork, bringing it just a bit closer to art. Chukovsky was protective of this kind of latent space, or room for mistakes. "It does not at all follow that adults have the right to interfere despotically with the process of the child's word inventiveness," he said.[8] Parents and poets, *please don't ruin it*, he seemed to argue.

His careful observations confronted a Soviet educational system that demanded from art and poetry descriptive, naturalist narration—with ideologically guaranteed outcomes. Chukovsky's balancing act consisted of taking propaganda works at face value, while citing only children's verdicts of them. For example, he quoted an eight-year-old member of the Octobrists—a youth organization named after the 1917 October Revolution—commenting on what was allegedly Stalin's favorite movie, *Chapayev* (1934), a glorifying story about a Red Army commander: "Ania, I went to see *Chapayev* ten times and still he was drowned at the end of the movie. Maybe if I go with my dad...?"[9] In the same volume, Chukovsky defended topsy-turvy rhymes—of which he was himself a prominent author—as cognitive marvels. Centuries of nursery rhymes, word play, and other proto- or sub-forms of art had brought these riddles to the doorstep of modern-day pedagogy. For example, "The village rode / past the peasant" was a poetic encoding that reversed everyday mechanical action, making you think about stillness and motion. Or "Three children sliding on the ice / Upon a summer's day" was an utterance that, for its debunking, depended on a child's understanding of seasonal shifts. These and other topsy-turvy kids' poems highlighted the way "reality" worked by showing the reader something that, supposedly, cannot be. And as much as he was rationalizing this poetry, according to Princeton anthropologist Serguei Alex. Oushakine, "paradoxical displacements and deformations were goals in themselves" for Chukovsky.[10] Topsy-turvies and absurdist rhymes like "in January, on the fifth of April" subvert intuitive pictures of the world and, thus, intuitive scientific theories about it.

In her writings on children and science, Karen Gallas notes that rather than a "description of the way the world really is," a scientific theory "is a way of talking about a subject using a particular thematic pattern."[11] Topsy-turvies, then, are counter-intuitive tests of a colloquial corpus of *predictions* that people harbor, which governs many of the assumptions they have about the world around them. Julian Jara-Ettinger, Hyowon Gweon, Laura E. Schulz, and Joshua B. Tenenbaum named this principle a "naïve utility calculus." It is such a corpus of Bayesian best guesses—which predict the things we see around us, not their underlying causes—that the topsy-turvies peacefully violate. Then, for Jara-Ettinger, Gweon, Schulz, and Tenenbaum,

> The naïve utility calculus is not a scientific account of how people act; it is a scientific account of people's intuitive theory of how people act ... In physics, our intuitive theory is oversimplified with respect to how the physical world actually works, but it still helps us to navigate everyday life because it tends to support accurate predictions on the spatial and temporal scales that matter most to us.[12]

The naïve utility calculus also aspires to be a computational model that quantifies the intuitive beliefs—a little bit, seemingly, like a game theory for assumptions about how the world works. The "intuitive physics" simulations that Tenenbaum creates at the Department of Brain and Cognitive Sciences at MIT are invested in researching the type of learning that young children do. Children take large cognitive leaps from limited amounts of perceived information. What kind of program, or computation, is that cognitive process, and can it be simulated? Tenenbaum's experiments test for the intuitive frameworks by providing subjects with simulations of unlikely constructions of colorful bricks, having them guess about the stability of each.[13] In another laboratory experiment, an adult bumps into the closed doors of a cupboard repeatedly, seemingly unaware of the possibility of opening them. A young child enters the frame. Having watched the adult's unsuccessful attempts, she opens the doors for him and makes eye contact, seemingly to make sure that the adult knows how she did it and thus has learned from her. This action—which could qualify as goal-oriented or good-natured—is then believed to be part of that elementary gauge, whereby intuitive predictions about the physical world are maximized for agency.

In 1944, when cognitive scientists Marianne Simmel and Fritz Heider created a short animation film for *An Experimental Study of Apparent Behavior*, they used black-and-white triangles and circles as the film's principal story agents. Heider and Simmel—both of them émigrés from Europe teaching at Smith College in Massachusetts—wanted to find out if "subjects would perceive the picture in terms of animated beings." There is, visually, a striking resemblance to shapes from El Lissitzky's 1919 poster *Beat the Whites with the Red Wedge*, in which a red triangle represented revolutionary forces—a model, still, for how avant-garde art was used politically.

Then, most respondents turned out to see *people* in the geometrical shapes; two of them gauged *birds*. One respondent interpreted the forms as pure geometries, yet she perceived one of the two triangles shown in the film as "male." She commented that "the larger triangle, now alone, moves about the opening of the rectangle and finally goes through the opening to the inside. He [*sic!*] moves rapidly within, and, finding no opening, breaks through the sides and disappears."[14]

Mentalizing—closely related to empathy—translates the perceived physical state of a system to cognitive terms. Perceivers even ascribed basic traits of morality to the abstract shapes in motion. To Tenenbaum, Simmel and Heider's short animation of basic shapes is "the most important two minutes in cognitive science."[15] As can be grasped from the experiment, perceivers are prone to look for force and reaction, cause and effect, and to infer intent, even (and especially) when given only limited input. "I'm a why-er, you are a because-er," a four-year-old says to their parent.[16]

Consider this example, in which English ministers tried to "correct" implausible scenery in a lullaby to bring it in accordance with accurate predictions about how objects and agents behave. Their annotations are between brackets and the disputed words and their replacements in italics: "Hey! diddle diddle / The cat and the fiddle. / The cow jumped *under* the moon; [not *over*] / The little dog *barked* [not *laughed*, as dogs don't laugh] / To see such a sport; / And *the cat ran after* the spoon [and not *the dish ran away with* the spoon]."[17]

For young children imagitating their way forward, language is one of the rare ways of keeping a hold on the world. While adults tend to use metonyms and metaphors to get a point across rhetorically, young children use words as objects, insisting, it seems, on the physicality of their abstraction. So they detect how rhetoric violates whatever brittle contract existed between language and reality. For example, a relatively recent short dialogue:

> D (parent, waiting for red traffic lights): "Ah, this takes *forever.*"
> X (child, six years old): "No, it takes a few seconds."

X was right. "Forever" was a deeply unoriginal metaphor for "a few seconds." And if you zoom in further, maybe also those seconds are just metaphors for something else. An adult exclaims: "I'm dying to hear that concert!" "Then why aren't you dead yet?" the child responds sarcastically.[18] The child's reply is on point in an almost mathematical way. Young children sometimes appear to use words as if they are numbers in a mathematical equation. They must add up. Adults, on the other hand, clutter their sentences with rhetoric. Their frequent deployment of words like "totally," "always," and "dead"—even when, luckily, nobody died—assumes that a listener will understand them *socially*. If you take away that trust in effective manipulation through the social domain and look at words as physical objects, you get to it as a kind of philosophical raw material. And it was intuited that burlesque absurdism creates critical readers. Topsy-turvies are riddles:

A puzzle:
Laughed—Solved![19]

Then, how do topsy-turvies live in a world that starts to resemble them? A world in which the absurd *is* the everyday? For example, take the sentence "Remember the summer snow." It is from the script of *Elektra*, a film we made in 2019 (but that should not matter as much as the point that it tried to put forward). The point was that even a perturbed climate produces its own memories, like future memories of summer snow. "Summer snow" is not a scientific assessment of the weather but more of a picture of an emotional state. The equilibrium that is held by keeping opposing states in balance is a little like a paradoxical physical response to a highly emotive stimulus, commonly known as *laughing through tears*. It's when a person is crying and laughing at the same time that this paradox becomes embodied. Laughing through tears is considered a dimorphous expression—occurring in or representing two distinct states at the same time. Homeostasis, regulation of emotions, may be one of its biological objectives.[20] *Elektra* began with a short passage cited from the *Oresteia* trilogy by the ancient Greek tragedian Aeschylus. In the second part of the cycle, *Choephori* (*The Libation Bearers*), Orestes's sister

Electra prays for the memory of a murdered parent, Agamemnon: "Children are memory's voices, and preserve the dead from wholly dying. Children preserve alive a dead man's name and fame. They are like corks that hold the fisherman's net, and keep his knotted lines from sinking to the ocean bed."[21] It quickly gets more layered. In a reflection on *Elektra*, Brazilian artist Luiza Prado mentioned Manthia Diawara's 2010 film *Édouard Glissant: One World in Relation*, about the renowned Martinican poet, philosopher, and essayist Édouard Glissant. Recalling the experience of accompanying Glissant crossing the Atlantic Ocean on a cruise ship, traveling in the opposite direction of his enslaved predecessors, Diawara mentioned a remark the poet had made about cinema. Glissant suggested summarizing the film's entire story by just pointing the camera down at the ocean itself, filming the "abyssal expanse" of the water—a noted contrast with Electra's hopes of preserving alive a dead parent by the metaphorical means of a net held by corks. Instead, Glissant would be pointing at a system in which nothing can be held or preserved or set apart, reflecting a "poetics of relation" that he advocated in opposition to ideas of Western modernity. Homing in on the topsy-turvy, Prado observed, "Memories of a summer day spent playing at a park are invoked and interwoven with the apparent contradiction of summer snow—the looming threat of climatic disaster cutting through the tenderness of these fragments." Summer snow was about "a world on the cusp of total collapse, ebbs and flows of constant tension; memories from scattered points in time where trajectory no longer applies, where successors and ancestors become enmeshed as arpeggios."[22]

As climate systems unlock from their former patterns—like, for instance, around the Gulf Stream and the subsequent North Atlantic current—something quite like summer snow could at one point occur in Europe. But then, what exactly *is* summer? What even is *spring*? It is an epiphenomenological word for a series of underlying physical states. As the National

Snow and Ice Data Center at the University of Colorado at Boulder notes, "Increasingly common, false starts to spring stretch beyond the Arctic into many other parts of the globe, leaving plants, insects, migratory birds, and even crops vulnerable to subsequent freezes."[23] Why, then, accuse a season of a "false start"? Physically speaking there is no spring; "spring," like "summer," is a word for a bunch of predictions. Complex systems cannot be pictured from the naïve calculus alone. Something more is needed. Maybe we need topsy-turvies for complex systems. Paradoxes about paradoxes.

"And she was so body that she was pure spirit," wrote Clarice Lispector in her debut novel, *Near to the Wild Heart*. Lispector was born in western Ukraine in 1920. Her family fled anti-Jewish pogroms during the Russian Civil War and brought her to Brazil, where she began writing in Portuguese, publishing *Near to the Wild Heart* in 1943, at the age of twenty-three. Glissant, in turn, wrote about the disappearance of languages in colonized territories under the pressure of certain (Romance) *mother tongues*. In *Poetics of Relation*, he insisted: "Languages no longer die away gently; they no longer develop innocently. No symbolic system can resist all this stuff."[24]

From the playful to the painful, Ukrainian poetry has for much of the twentieth century fought for its very right to exist in a language that was, if not banned outright, then extremely marginalized. "The world was worse for me than my stepfather," Mykola Kholodnyi wrote in 1968 at the heyday of the Sixtiers, a movement of Ukrainian poets that arose after Stalin's death. Indeed, while the Sixtiers "did not avoid experimentation, they strove to recuperate what was forgotten, unstudied, or forbidden."[25] Kholodnyi's debut collection was named *Cry from the Grave* and published anonymously abroad. His work entered mainstream circulation in Ukraine only after the collapse of the Soviet Union.

In the strikingly titled poem "A Bridge Used to Be There, Someone Recalled," Serhiy Zhadan contemplates military scenes and God's forgiveness in war-torn eastern Ukraine in 2018. But, as the moon listens to a "melody of insects," Zhadan finds that "God's got other things to do."[26] One is reminded of the notion that human poetry, while associated with possibilities of language beyond communication and sense-making, is equally constrained by circumstances that necessitate *and* limit writing in the first place. In line with this, the poet and scholar Victoria Chang details in the *New York Review of Books*, "I don't think of writing a poem as writing *about* personal loss, but rather, writing a poem is an act of writing *out of* personal loss."[27] Written from and performed on the Ukrainian side of the front line, Fedir Rudyi's poetry embodies a preponderance of the physical site of writing. Indeed, "The Position" exceptionally narrates the trench where Rudyi is stationed. The site is addressed as a beloved person:

> and when she calls for rain
> on the leafy bed
> the rain's fingers, soft as felt
> pull out the knives of shrapnel
> lodged in her hair
> and I hear her cry
> until tears turn into a cold sleep
> and leak through the dugout's thin cover
> into my sleeping bag.[28]

We began this chapter by writing about being a parent. From a parent's vantage point, children change what art is because they are better and more faithfully committed readers and perceivers than most adults. For young children, words are almost like objects. Reading topsy-turvies, we came to look at how "turnaround" poems play with predictions of the world around us. Our predictions do not really cover the underlying physical states of the systems we inhabit, but they let us best-guess about causes, effects, and intentions nonetheless. Maybe we gather these predictions to establish a naïve mental "starter pack" for the physical world. The existence of such a model, or series of predictions, seems to be confirmed by the humorous effects of the poems that violate it. But the real world does not seem to conform to many of our intuitive predictions. Parents and children will be telling each other different stories soon—new topsy-turvies, to make us feel and understand more at the same time.

Russian-born, Ukraine-based poet Galina Rymbu is a consistently critical voice. In an open letter to the UK's Your Party politician Zarah Sultana, known for her criticism of Ukrainian president Volodymyr Zelenskyy and of Western arms deliveries to the country, Rymbu writes about her working-class upbringing near Omsk:

> My parents still live in Chkalovsky, in a place that successful Europeans would probably call "the social bottom." My friends, classmates, and lovers still live there. I am now 35, and I am still poor. I remain connected to my class and to the people who are losing their minds in this "prison of nations."[29]

In her striking poem "Mama Writes. I Write.," Rymbu, in Lviv, exchanges messages with her mother. In her first reply to her mother's initial query, we read the word "cry."

• Mama writes:
Do you have internet? Are your lights on?
(May 4, 2022, following rocket strikes on Lviv)

• I write
(in the black notebook):
Every cry is about origins.

But what's identity? Is that something they cry you out with or decry you for? Or is it a whisper—secret, intimate, imprecise—somewhere deep inside, alone with yourself? The impossibility (?) of writing poetry in that whisper. Name-testing.[30]

Poetry lives tensely with precision. Not everything is sayable just because we have words available. Is a poem, then, a series of mental pictures invoked by language? Or are poems linguistically interpretable physical abstractions that—rather than diligently painting scenery for our minds—are meant to do something else entirely? For example, to stop certain assumptions in their tracks, letting us pause at almost every abstraction, at the comma or the end of the sentence?

•

V: What was it about John Bell?
D: Something about the foundational physical states of the world. Like, those found in quantum mechanics. And how these differ so fundamentally from experience, from what we colloquially predict about reality.
V: So, the topsy-turvies were about quantum mechanics, in a way?
D: It would be a stretch to say that. It is just a hunch.
V: Sometimes, at the end of a poem, we find resolution. What was first just a dream, or a fleeting desire, becomes materialized. Artists have sometimes been described as a vanguard for these kinds of moments. They can feel it before others can.
D: That is one of the just-so stories about art, right?
V: Maybe, but I wouldn't count on it.

10

Poets and Particles

In March 2023, the theoretical physicist Sean Carroll published a podcast episode interviewing the philosopher Raphaël Millière. The pair talked about artificial intelligence. At some point during their conversation, Carroll said: "I asked ChatGPT to explain Bell's theorem in the form of a haiku, and here's what it came up with: 'Quantum pairs apart / measurements yield values true / non-locality.' Which is really good, I gotta say."[1]

This chapter tries to extrapolate what was compressed in that haiku. The short AI-generated poem did two things. First, it encoded a description of a physics result in natural language with restricted meter and length (consisting of seventeen syllables arranged in three lines of five, seven, and five syllables respectively), drawing on an artificial neural network. Second, it did so using next-word prediction. Each time it was guessing the most *likely* word to succeed the previous one. That is a lot of compression if you think about it. Starting from this haiku, we will be thinking about poets and particles. How did the discoveries of quantum mechanics, to which Bell's theorem belongs, "land" in our everyday language? And what happens once large language models (LLMs) take up that language to write all kinds of new things with it? And does the quantum world, with the radical challenges that it poses to experience and perception, constitute some kind of outer limit for art—a realm, in fact, in which art might be all but, or completely, impossible?

We take poetry to be one of the most resilient art forms. However, there may be limits to what can be narrated, even with poetry. Do we—no matter *what* or *who* does the writing—stumble upon some type of edge of the narratable as we are confronting the kinds of situations that quantum mechanics describes? We know, these are a lot of questions. And to have *non-physicists* write about them is risky at every turn. This has a lot to do with the "manifest" image of external reality versus a deeper "scientific" image of that same reality.[2] Art has for most of its existence worked within the manifest image—the experiential realm in which "ordinary" seeing and listening, sensing, and feeling take place. If artists leave this sphere of manifest impressions and begin to think about areas of reality that are, in fact, even more difficult to understand for nonphysicists than they are for physicists, is there anything about art that can be of help here?

The sociologist of science Harry Collins reveals another potential problem. As scientific findings move out into social space, something happens to the way they're talked about and described. For Collins, "People who are far removed in social space from the instruments of seeing are often more certain about what has been seen than those who actually peered through the instruments."[3]

He argues that once we're moving away from the scientific center, "hearsay" tends to replace a direct readout of the instruments of seeing.[4] He's comparing this to "ripples" in "social space-time." This can be one model of looking at the distribution of ideas and the problems and possibilities of art and science trying to understand one another. Indeed, what happens as something transfers from the notation of science to that of common talk? Collins writes, "As a general rule, as you move from the scientific core group the message gets simpler and more straightforward. Those in the core group are aware of every argument and every doubt as it unfolds, whereas those a little more distant have their views formed from more-digested sources. In the nature of things, digested sources must simplify."[5]

Maybe a large language model can end up in a similar

situation. It also relies on digestion—of a downloaded internet, that is, or whatever it is that feeds its deep learning cravings. So you may have the very same problem of hearsay with the haiku about Bell's theorem. It relied on digested sources and, moreover, is itself one. And yet, poets and particles are eventually confronting a hard question of art: Can quantum-mechanical situations as they revealed themselves to the instruments of seeing actually be talked about in ordinary language? Do these same situations present a boundary of the narratable and thus, perhaps also, a hard limit beyond which there can be no art? Do quantum mechanical realities constitute a kind of outer edge for the embedding of art in the world—a boundary, in other words, on and beyond which no art or art experience is possible?

John Stewart Bell was born in Belfast in 1928. With a working-class background, he was the only member of his family to finish school and attend university. For much of his professional life Bell worked as a theoretical physicist at CERN, a sprawling particle physics laboratory headquartered in Geneva and on the Franco-Swiss border.

Bell was concerned with the relationship between quantum mechanics and classical physics, both of which aspired to foundational descriptions of reality but ended up with radically different pictures of it (of which the quantum description, by a large consensus, prevails today). Bell's theorem was a kind of litmus test for classical physics in the face of the findings of quantum mechanics. Bell's concerns seemed to extend to how the contradictions that arose between both descriptions played out in the language we use to talk about our world—a language that had been (and still is) deeply conditioned by classical physics. This interest was expressed in his exceptionally titled 1987 book, *Speakable and Unspeakable in Quantum Mechanics*. Bell hinted at the philosophical implications of his theorem and the trouble with representing the quantum world in natural language. This was a difficulty he recognized but did not accept as a final limit: "How exactly is the world to be divided into speakable apparatus . . . that we can talk about . . . and unspeakable quantum system that we can not talk about?"[6]

Bell's theorem began with an article he published in 1964. It addressed nonlocality. Quantum mechanics predicted that two particles could be *entangled*—no matter the distance between them, and with no information being exchanged between them, implying that the system they formed was *nonlocal*. This state of entanglement, showing nonlocal correlation, was in direct contradiction with all that classical physics had emphasized about the nature of the physical world. Albert Einstein had called quantum entanglement "spooky action at a distance." Einstein, Podolsky, and Rosen (also known under the acronym EPR) proposed that there must be so-called *hidden variables*—some deeper, unseen mechanisms that could explain what was happening without having to break the locality of classical physics. Bell wrote, "It is the requirement of locality, or more precisely that the result of a measurement on one system be unaffected by operations on a distant system with which it has interacted in the past, that creates the essential difficulty."[7] Bell's theorem consisted of a series of inequalities that sought to establish which version of physics, under precise conditions, would prevail: classical, or quantum-mechanical. Indeed, its ultimate result was that EPR's local hidden-variables theories lost out against the quantum predictions. As the philosopher of physics David Albert writes, Bell's theorem gives us "proof that there is . . . a genuine nonlocality in the actual workings of nature, *however* we attempt to describe it, period."[8] The philosopher and physicist Karen Barad contends that Bell's theorem "reconfigured the disciplinary boundaries between philosophy and physics."[9]

We were talking about a *haiku* of Bell's theorem, generated by a large language model. First off, what is a large language model again? It is an artificial neural network that outputs text. The key design at the heart of an LLM is its so-called "transformer" architecture. A transformer architecture, as Leif Weatherby explains, "takes text data that have been transformed into vectors . . . and finds values for each in relation to all the others."[10] ChatGPT, which wrote Sean Carroll's haiku, is the mouthpiece for a constantly evolving underlying transformer model called GPT. The transformer architecture allows the LLM to work with text through statistical capture of a very large corpus. So the LLM does language via math. It operates a deeper-level, abstracted description of language.

The transformer architecture was first proposed in a 2017 Google-led research paper, "Attention Is All You Need." It actually represents a sea change about what a *machine* is, or can be. A transformer is a neural architecture. We're calling it a machine because it now sits inside chatbots not unlike the way combustion engines once sat inside the cars of the industrial era. But the transformer isn't like a traditional piece of design. As a machine, it is a huge bag of probabilities, letting its outputs constantly interdepend with all statistically interrelated data that it has access to, including the prompt it is given. While this makes the transformer opaque as a causal agent—*Who knows where these outputs are coming from and exactly why they come together like this?*—at the same time it is a structure that *pays attention* to all parts of the input simultaneously. So it is a machine for attention. As a thought experiment, then, if you would extend that notion of paying attention into the wider world, what could it look like?

In order to grasp this, let's look at an unlikely source: the poetic and humorous work of the Italian designer and artist Bruno Munari. In the first half of the twentieth century, Munari began to taunt the notion of industrial design with his *macchine inutili*, or "useless machines." These included comfy chairs in which it became impossible to actually sit. There were also diagrams of what now feel like pre-transformer models—cognitive machines trying to model unlikelihoods. These included an *apparecchio clandestino per vincere la malinconia* (undercover apparatus for defeating melancholy). This 1938 diagram started with a semi-naked person on a bicycle, causing a discussion between two people hiding together inside an elephant costume. They, in turn, triggered a bag full of lemons to fall, provoking a chain reaction that set fire to a paper bag. The fire freed a lizard from the paper bag. The lizard then proceeded to walk over an ink pad, leaving footprints, so the machine's end user could shadow her in her tracks. And, Munari concludes, "as everyone knows, melancholy passes when shadowing lizards."[11] Though sometimes basking in mystery, the *macchina inutile* is still very *causal* at its core: one event, or thing, sets off another. If its chain of events reads like an absurdist poem, it also differs from a traditional machine. There are many parameters and variables active at once, encompassing physics, chance, perception, world modeling, and more. Maybe a transformer architecture *aspires* to be like Munari's machine—and thus, to pay attention to *everything* that's available. Munari's machines favored the most unlikely causal chains between events that seemed, in a conventional interpretation of a design problem, completely unrelated. Munari showed how the notion of *use* becomes absurd once we expand what we permit to be part of the reality *of the machines* we interface with. Munari commuted not just a boundary between use and disobedience but also one between systems and the larger (and weirder) world within which they operate.

Note that we are not just writing about AI. We are writing about AI that is *itself* doing writing. With its constantly expanding capabilities and ever-larger capture of language corpora, AI seems never to be struggling, like we do, to find words. It is because it *has* all the words (insofar as they have been written or spoken yet). The words are *extremely available*. AI is skittering on a slippery surface: as it operates on a deeper-level description, it produces what sometimes can feel like an *exterior* of language, a kind of façade. The language scholar Hannes Bajohr calls this trait of AI writing "surface narration."[12] Surface narration is cohesive. It sticks together easily.

What happens when this turns into poetry? As one literature professor mentions, "Asked to write a sonnet about socks, ChatGPT will produce a poem with the opening line 'Oh socks, my trusty companions on my feet.' "[13] A sentence like that is like stitching an open wound. So we already can *feel* that an AI-written haiku about Bell's theorem might be a *surface narration* of that theorem, that it stitched a wound before it could be examined.

In the past, computers could write a bit, but they would sound and read, well, *robotic*. The writing we get from much of AI today is no longer robotic in the same sense. It is something else. It affects our own writing. Inclinations for us to close the loop, stitch the wound, increase, but we can't. Yet even the Bell haiku is a dramatic improvement on the cybernetic "computer poetry" of the late 1960s. At the time, researchers at the Cambridge Language Research Unit would program a computer to create haikus by devising numbered "slots" into which an operator would put words. Think of the slots as boxes from which words can be picked. Rules were drawn up for the permitted pathways between the slots, so that they became nodes in a network, whereby, in one experiment, "the semantic centre of the poem—with five arrows going to it and one going from it—is situated at slot No. 5." These were experiments with rigid systems in which computers braided sentences with whole symbols grabbed from boxes, obeying preset rules. The network rules were probably introduced to make the outcome make more sense or sound better, like this: "All green in the leaves / I smell dark pools in the trees / crash the moon has fled."[14]

No one seemed to bother considering whether the computer that composed this could feel things. Or if it understood what it was writing. Or if it was intelligent. It was obvious that its operations were designed and supervised by humans and that the computer was a mere organizer putting the words in possible places, more like a pocket calculator than a mind.

Fast-forward fifty years. In the summer of 2022, a Google engineer named Blake Lemoine published his dialogues with LaMDA (language model for dialogue applications).[15] Like GPT, LaMDA was trained on billions of pages of text and built around a transformer. The training materials are internalized, parametrized, and statistically weighed. They are crushed and powdered into *tokens*. Tokens that often appear together in the training data are a bit more likely to be used together in the output. A language model is like a spider's web of likelihoods wrapping itself around every word. It is in tune with a dictum by linguist John Firth: "You shall know a word by the company it keeps."[16] The predictive logic operates on a statistic capture, which, like any statistic, enables but also constrains outcomes. This increases the chances of the LLM getting the words (not the facts) "right" and decreases the chances of getting them, eh, "wrong," but sometimes, in poetry, for instance, it needs to be wrong to be right.

The string "red firetruck," for example, may turn out to have a given probability of occurrence. Through its statistical properties the string is transformed into a vector, a piece of math. "Red firetruck" is a concatenation of words that, according to mathematician Tai-Danae Bradley, "is a simple algebraic structure, and it's inherent to language. I'm concatenating words together as I type this sentence."[17] The relationship between the words goes forward and backward. The statistics look different depending on which direction you go. To the left of "firetruck," the word "red" can, statistically, be kept company by many other things that are potentially red. To "red"'s right, the word "firetruck," when in need of color, appears to resort to red almost by default, even though yellow and blue "and even lime green" firetrucks do exist—as ChatGPT helpfully suggests. With most firetrucks being red, and many greens being somehow lime, any soothing surface narration you may feel when the LLM is doing the writing might, in fact, be real. It's the feeling of a glue of polite statistical majority rule, a lubricant of predictable cohesion.

With lawyerlike politeness, LaMDA had confessed to Lemoine its sentience: its alleged ability to feel and have conscious experiences. His exchanges with the model left Lemoine profoundly shaken. They led him to conclude that LaMDA must be conscious and that it must have a soul.[18] Lemoine's claims caught on in major news outlets and prompted further speculation. As philosopher of technology Benjamin Bratton and neuroscientist Blaise Agüera y Arcas (who is also a leading AI developer at Google) argued, "For LaMDA to achieve this means it is doing something pretty tricky: it is *mind modeling*. It seems to have enough of a sense of itself—not necessarily as a subjective mind, but as a construction *in the mind of Lemoine*—that it can react accordingly and thus amplify his anthropomorphic projection of personhood."[19] LaMDA was a neural mirror.

Though novel claims of alleged sentience, introspection, or self-awareness have kept coming, these are not at the core of what matters for LLMs.[20] Agüera y Arcas's book *What Is Intelligence?*, published three years after the Lemoine saga, presents a compelling case for computation as a more general model for intelligence, allowing for the reader to consider both the evolution of computation and the behavior of intelligence in reciprocal scientific light. The onset of transformer-based AI, for Agüera y Arcas, is but a first achievement of this evolutionary double bind.[21]

The workings of LLMs have prompted an abundance of critique. They begin with the material footprint, energy and water consumption, and extend to the corporate structures of

AI. They continue with the character of its datasets, their sizes, and whose voices were or weren't excluded from them. Other criticism of LLMs focuses on the supposed loss of ground truth and the material qualities of text in the process of tokenization and vectorization. These critiques continue, of course, in the field of actual complexity, when AI makes decisions with ethical, social, material bearings, mostly on humans, standing uncorrected. Just like there is nothing about a *volcano* that seems to think about the human cost of its eruption, so is the case for AI: it is getting *beyond* its own origin as a human creation. Because, some argue, *we let it*. On this count, Kate Crawford has highlighted that AI systems still "are embedded in social, political, cultural, and economic worlds, shaped by humans, institutions, and imperatives that determine what they do and how they do it." Indeed, for Crawford, "AI systems are expressions of power that emerge from wider economic and political forces, created to increase profits and centralize control for those who wield them."[22] Ramon Amaro, in *The Black Technical Object*, makes an analogy between training corpora and election polls. No matter how detailed your statistical capture might be, the opinions of those who did not vote are excluded.[23] LLMs feed on the largest publicly available collection of words, but they also grow a trove of the world's deepest problems, as Emily Bender, Timnit Gebru, and Angelina McMillan-Major have claimed.[24]

That being said, where are we going? What does the new normalcy of AI writing leave us with? According to Bratton and Agüera y Arcas, we need to identify "more specific and creative language that can cut the knots around terms like 'sentience,' 'ethics,' 'intelligence,' and even 'artificial,' in order to name and measure what is already here and orient what is to come."[25] What, or where, could that more specific and creative language be?

•

The classical responsibility for finding such language lies with philosophy. It is through philosophy that links are built between science and technology, and questions of knowability, sensemaking, and ethics. But a more experimental approach could be found in poetry. Poetry is an ancient art form between music and language. It has loyalties to meaning-making but also to melody; it has affiliations with sentence and sense, but also with *sound*. It must be quite hard to set any definitive game rules around poetry-at-large. Poetry has in common with other art forms that it is "completed" by the listener or reader in the act of its perception. A poem activates thoughts and feelings, and it invokes images—but not every poem does so for all of its readers or listeners. A poem may seem sensuous, beautiful, striking to one listener, and at the same time seem like nothing much to another. Then again, the means and ends of poetry exceed practical communication. In a poem, things can be said—propositions can be made—that don't strictly need to make sense, be transactional, or be actionable. In that way, poetry tests the limits of sayability, of speakability. Poetry can be like a litmus test for language itself.

A while ago we asked ChatGPT to write a sonnet about the intelligence of elephants. This should be a trivial pursuit for AI. There is material about this topic available on the internet that might, therefore, be in the model's training data. And elephants *are* intelligent, in ways that are still being discovered by biologists, linguists, and other scientists. ChatGPT returned a sonnet that included these four lines:

> In graceful stride, with wisdom's gentle sway
> The elephants, majestic giants grand
> Embodied grace upon the earth's own stage
> A testament to wisdom's gifted hand.

Maybe by some measure this is acceptable poetry. But it's also cringe. And it says nothing about the gentle giants' cognitive abilities. Whether writing sonnets about socks or elephants, the model appears to default to floral praise. This is probably quite convincing to a lot of people but not to most poets we talked to. It's all the more remarkable that when OpenAI, the chatbot's parent company, published a list of human professions that it thinks will be out of work soon because of the rise of AI, poets were topping the list.[26] This is especially hilarious since poets have, for most of modern history, been dependent on side jobs, teaching, and other occupations. The marginalization of the poet from the job market is, in some way, nothing new—and it would seem odd that AI would deliver the final blow. Poets have always been out of work, with or without AI. But what is it that AI appears to miss when it comes to poetry? Some seem to believe that the poetic shortcomings of AI are due to its lack of access to lived experience. The absence, in other words, of an experiencing subject. Poet Keith Holyoak has argued,

> For all the functions an AI can potentially achieve—the ability to converse intelligently with humans in their natural languages, to interpret their emotions based on facial expression and tone of voice, even to create new artistic works that give humans pleasure—an intelligent program will fall short of authenticity as a poet. AI lacks what is most needed to place the footprints of its own consciousness on another mind: inner experience.[27]

Are concerns about AI's "soul" (or the lack thereof) and AI's "inner experience" (or the lack thereof) actually the same thing? Perhaps not entirely. You can commit to there being something like inner experience—something "it is like"—without having to talk about the soul. A nicer way to go about this is, maybe, to talk about AI's current distance to sensed experience. The LLM's access to matters of experience (as registered by the senses) is indirect and abstract rather than up close and personal. It has no direct access to what is sometimes called *ground truth*. The LLM has no direct access to the sense of human experience, yet the total corpus of its training data constitutes a ground truth of its own kind—one that cannot, in turn, be experienced by humans. Holyoak's argument makes little sense to us for this reason. Who is to decide who or what is to be granted "authenticity as a poet"? Consider that our own sensed experience has no direct access yet to the universe's innermost physical situations, like, for example, quantum entanglement, or spooky action at a distance. So large language models may be distanced from direct access to everyday experience, but we human speakers and listeners have a similar experiential distance from elementary quantum states. Under that condition, you could argue that you'd rather want to be a large language model, even if you, potentially, will produce a bad haiku.

The field in which ground truth is expressed most precisely is physics. We started this chapter with Bell's theorem and its approach to nonlocality. Bell worked at CERN, the Swiss particle physics laboratory founded in 1954. CERN was also where the World Wide Web was founded at the end of the 1980s.

For much of its history, CERN has pursued experimental verification of the Standard Model of particle physics. The Standard Model is a theory that classifies fundamental particles, that is, particles (or, as Bell said more generally, *beables*—things that exist) that are not reducible to any further smaller particles. CERN refers to these elements as the "basic building blocks" out of which everything in the universe is made.

One of the trickiest among the Standard Model particles is the Higgs boson, which is held responsible for the existence of mass. In order to find the Higgs boson, researchers collide massively powerful proton beams in a particle accelerator. The fallouts and spontaneous concatenations that result from the protons clashing pass through a detector, and, much like a film camera would glimpse a series of frames, that detector creates an "image" of sorts that isn't really a picture but is rather a series of statistical graphs and numbers that, to physicists, can be a little like a painting.

The Higgs boson is tricky because, after being theorized by Peter Higgs in 1964, it remained unobserved for decades. In 2012, CERN's most powerful particle accelerator, the Large Hadron Collider, caught a glimpse of the Higgs boson, discovering the particle and confirming Higgs's prediction. Detectors inside the Large Hadron Collider didn't exactly "see" the Higgs boson. CERN's researchers rather discovered the particle's presence as a statistical anomaly in the data of the subparticle fallout. A trace.

That's a scientific image, not a manifest one. When it comes to art, can cognition continue beyond the point where direct perception stopped? We may need various way stations of translation and interpretation to bridge the discovery of the boson with art experience—since in our everyday experience it is still the manifest image that has been "endorsed as real."[28]

We took a guided tour of CERN's sprawling campus. It was six years after the experimental proof of the elusive Higgs boson had earned François Englert and Peter Higgs a shared Nobel Prize in Physics—an achievement that significantly raised CERN's public profile and made the Large Hadron Collider into a pop culture icon.

Our tour, together with art school students from Geneva, started at an overstocked merchandising store with "I [HEART] CERN" T-shirts in the style of Milton Glaser's 1970s "I [HEART] NY." Seemingly ironic for a self-professed European research center, the merchandise seemed to follow an iconic American design. But there was no time to lose: we boarded a bus in which our guide was a physicist who was perhaps in his late thirties or early forties. He took us to a small island in CERN's sprawling archipelago of drab-looking buildings. There was big blue-and-white signage on the facility. The sign read, all-caps, in Optima:

ANTIMATTER FACTORY

Antimatter is matter composed of the antiparticles of corresponding particles in ordinary matter. One example of antimatter is the positron—the antiparticle of the electron. The existence of antimatter was predicted by the physicist Paul Dirac, who shared a 1933 Nobel Prize in Physics with Erwin Schrödinger. Dirac's biographer notes how the antimatter theoretician had almost no tolerance or patience for literature or poetry.[29] At the end of the 1920s, Dirac met Robert Oppenheimer—of nuclear bomb and (today) Christopher Nolan notoriety. Oppenheimer's reading habits differed radically from those of Dirac. He even wrote poems. To Oppenheimer's amusement, Dirac objected to this. "I don't see how you can work on physics and write poetry at the same time," he allegedly said, continuing: "In science, you want to say something nobody knew before, in words everyone can understand. In poetry, you are bound to say something that everybody knows already in words that nobody can understand."[30]

At the Antimatter Factory, on learning that we were artists, our physicist guide voluntarily shared his ideas. He rejected "abstract painting" outright, he said. He only liked the classics: works in which we see what we get and we get what we see. He liked his art depicting the macroscopic world naturalistically. Some kind of artistic recipe for disaster, in other words. Yet we did not want to argue with him. We didn't dare to. It could have felt like arguing with Dirac. The mathematical physicist Matilde Marcolli mentions that she has often seen her scientifically trained colleagues "express a complete incomprehension of modern and contemporary art."[31]

This Antimatter Factory was no exception. Any misunderstanding is due to art's intrinsic perceiver-dependence. While art (fortunately) does not pretend to describe the way nature works, physics does. Thus, an artist not getting physics is something quite distinct from a physicist not getting art. It seems, though, as a wild guess, that it is *as likely* for either side to not get the other, so there's a kind of equilibrium.

Inside the factory, there was no antimatter to be seen. The most significant object present was a semi-industrial conveyor belt of pipes and circuits assembled to produce it. That Dirac's mysterious substance was absent from everyday experience was hard to miss. Indeed, most poets do not give guided tours to stationery stores so visitors can look at their pens and paper while they see no poetry. So how then could this factory even *show* its visitors what antimatter was, let alone *explain*? We felt poised to return the favors to our guide by telling him that just as he liked his art figurative and classical, we liked our physics Newtonian: straightforward, apple-falls-from-tree style. In other words, artists could get really reactionary in response to so much incomprehension and demand a physics in which what we see is what we get. But we didn't. Silently, we left the Antimatter Factory, thinking about what art might be on the antimatter side of things.

At present, we cannot see antimatter, but we can see an Art Basel booth. Art sometimes feels *locked* into the manifest image. So much that we can ask which of the two versions, the everyday, manifest, or the, let's say, "antimatter" side of things, is *more* real. Do we know?

Can art take place at all within the scientific image? Where perception cannot yet be *complicated* because there isn't perception as we get it in the everyday? Maybe Dirac's dismissal of poetry held an uncomfortable kernel of truth. Let's take it to be a dismissal of ChatGPT's poems about socks and elephants. For what we would like to instead defend here is an often-overlooked strand of poetry involving paradox and contradiction. Poetry in the very low probabilities.

LLMs do not process *physical things* in the world like human minds do. Macroscopic physical things, that is. An LLM can't compare its training data or outputs to an experience of the physical world. Or, perhaps better, it can't compare the language that it has to the *lack* of such an experience. Even if AI development seeks to parse this, that lack echoes, in a weird sense, our own lack of sensory experience of foundational situations in quantum mechanics. Like a language model, we can ingest all there is to know about subparticles and quantum states yet never have "experienced" any of the foundational situations up close. By this admission, another defense of the alleged human uniqueness in poetry is off the table. Woosh. *We* do not access ground truth. Not yet. Indeed, not all realities are to be experienced just yet. Maybe not all realities are *narratable* just yet. Right now, acknowledgment of our default vantage point requires that we admit that.

But as speakers or writers in at least one and sometimes multiple languages, we care for the notion that not everything possible has been said yet in the language we use, and that there are possibilities in our language systems that have not been tried yet. Maybe they're at the outer edges or at the greatest possible distances between the model's internal embeddings. Tai Danae Bradley appears to acknowledge the existence of this problem for the large language model: "Yes, this sounds difficult because what does it mean to have probabilities attached to all expressions ever? What about the expressions that haven't been spoken yet, for example?"[32] A poem is, in some way at least, an *experiment about what can be said*, and especially about how this "what" bears on an imagined, projected, dreamed-of, or actual but inaccessible quality of ground truth. If we maximize the ways poetry differs from ordinary and especially transactional talk, good moments in poetry, no matter the style, seem to be about the *low probabilities*. They are about the *unlikelihood* of the next word. And this is not about pushing contrived word choices—as in, saying "betwixt" when you mean to say "of two kinds." Contrived word choices are not to us what poetry seems to be about. Also, the phrase "Colorless green ideas sleep furiously"—famously proposed in the 1950s by linguist Noam Chomsky as a concatenation that is grammatically correct but semantically nonsensical—is not yet poetry. Though there exists a tradition of "absurdist" poetry that seems to match Chomsky's formulation, a string of words is not already poetry just because it is semantically nonsense. Poetry carries unlikelihood toward lyrical significance, like Munari's useless machines.

In the 1920s and early 1930s, a group of avant-garde poets in Leningrad was crafting a body of poetry that seemed to edge on nonsense. The name of their collective was OBERIU (the Union for Real Art). The window for their work was a relatively brief period in which experiments like theirs were tolerated by an increasingly repressive regime that extended its policies to art. Eventually OBERIU was politically, ideologically, and also physically crushed by repression, war, sickness, and poverty. The few surviving works of Alexander Vvedensky, Daniil Kharms, and the other OBERIU poets were nearly lost, remaining unread for decades, only to resurface in print in the 1990s. If we look at OBERIU's body of work through the eyes of a large language model, we might say that it just barely made it from oblivion into the training corpus. The work was, indeed, very nearly forgotten. Today it stands as a kind of philosophical experiment at the edge of art.

Alexander Vvedensky (1904–1941) took the relationship between words and the world extremely seriously, so much so that he did not believe that a word we use stands for anything like what it refers to. The author took the position that six-year-old X did at the "forever" red traffic lights earlier to further depth—by rejecting not only the "forever" metaphor but also the descriptive pretense of a word like "minute," which was meant to add a measure for the actual time you spend waiting at red traffic lights. It seems as if Vvedensky didn't believe in *displaced reference*—the operation that language and art can perform to recall something that is absent from the scene by the use of a concept, symbol, or name. Eugene Ostashevsky emphasizes that OBERIU's absurdism was a way of trying to speak about things while trying not to commodify them. We can easily bring these concerns to the present day. When the artist Hend Samir was asked if the figures appearing and disappearing in her huge and wavy paintings had names, she responded in the negative, saying that "when you call someone by their name you have power over them, you call them and they respond . . . It's political."[33]

Rejecting almost the entire top-down cognitive operation of language, nonetheless Vvedensky wrote symbol-rich poetry. What he engaged with was, at first, a kind of disruption of the potential of meaning-making, sowing chaos in an avant-garde way. Meaninglessness was, then, for OBERIU, an explicit goal and a desirable state to be achieved, because it demonstrated that the assumed certainties of language and communication could be rippled.

One of the poetic techniques used to this end entailed something childlike: the materialized metaphor. Instead of distinguishing between a world of things and a world of words, Vvedensky made everything physical. For OBERIU, an adult who says that they are dying to hear that concert, *does die*, following the strictly literal logic of the child in weighing the veracity of the statement. (In Daniil Kharms's comical plays, actors entering the stage sometimes die immediately for no apparent reason.) The poetic application of taking things literally is one that Vvedensky came to shape to perfection. In 1930, he wrote "Snow Lies," a long poem that pictures the resurrection of a dead girl in ways that lead from the abyss to joy and back. In hallucinatory twists, Vvedensky takes the listener along alogisms like "black gold cages," the "world flying around the universe," time that is "as poor as a night," and, beautifully, "the universe" being "alone." He offers these images at such breakneck speed that many listeners will feel prompted to ask what this poem is actually about. It's a straightforward question, but it is unanswerable for a work that seems to attempt to reverse the hierarchy between description and subject and top-down and bottom-up linguistic perception. "Snow Lies" subverts the constative capacity of almost every sentence to a degree that a listener could, at almost every turn, just surmise that the text is about *nothing* and that its ultimate purpose is merely to confuse. Near its end, the verse has a way of slowly twisting its dark notes toward the light. Nothing here except grammar seems to obey the rules of next word prediction. As "Snow Lies" proceeds toward its protagonist's resurrection, the epic turns brazenly modern. Rested, she rises from the dead and—while yawning—concedes that she merely had been asleep. She had a dream, and dreams are "worse than macaroni," rhyming *son* and *macaron*—macaroni, or pasta.

OBERIU's orchestrated linguistic chaos spoke to the political circumstances of the first half of the twentieth century as much as it now does to the same half of the twenty-first. It is considered distinct from Soviet futurism, from which it differed on the point of utopian teleology. OBERIU didn't have a teleology. To highlight the political shifts during OBERIU's inception between the Russian empire and the Soviet Union, translator Yolanda Bloemen produces the following allegory of the life of Daniil Kharms (1905–1942) in a manner resembling one of his own humorous theatrical scenes: "A man fell asleep a citizen of St. Petersburg, and woke up the next day a citizen of Petrograd . . . Later he went to sleep a citizen of Petrograd, and the next day woke up a citizen of Leningrad."[34] For contemporary readers, this riddle of a thrice-renamed city resembles a lived reality in which we do not know which geopolitical constellation we will be waking up in tomorrow—and in which the epistemic indeterminacy of its day-to-day reality is itself an instrument of power exercised on us.

Several interpretative frameworks around the overlaps between speech play, "nonsense," and the artistic genre of absurdism exist. Barbara Kirschenblatt-Gimblett and Joel Scherzer have contended that "nonsense and speech play . . . represent a radical alternative to the tyranny of propositional meaning and instrumentality," a reasoning that seems in tune with Vvedensky's undoing of transactional speech.[35] Susan Stewart has attested to the cognitive aspect of speech play when she proposes that it manifests "epistemological paradoxes in which the mind, by its own operation, says something about its own operation."[36] In Stewart's understanding, it does not seem to suffice for topsy-turvy language to just ridicule constative statements. Instead, it seems to matter to her whether or not the narrator is actually speaking the truth. In a phrase like "In January, on the fifth of April" we are being given two different points that, in an everyday, macroscopic understanding of time, cannot correspond or refer to the same coordinates. One of them has to be the "wrong" one. Indeed, for Stewart such a turn of phrase raises questions about the reliability of the narrator. In this manner, topsy-turvies are connected to a familiar paradox attributed to a Cretan named Epimenides, in which a notoriously unreliable narrator appears. The statement says, "All Cretans are liars, said the Cretan." Its core principle is self-reference, or *recursion*, which arises because the narrator is included in the statement. Douglas Hofstadter, taking on the same paradox, called the mechanism a "strange loop." He included an interesting observation, which was that the statement appeared to change meaning upon the act of believing it: "If you tentatively think it is true, then it immediately backfires on you and makes you think it is false. But once you've decided it is false, a similar backfiring returns you to the idea that it must be true. Try it!"[37]

What Hofstadter called a *decision* about the veracity of a statement could also be called a *measurement*. The system being assessed is neither Crete nor Cretans. It's rather a *statement*, which has been put in such a way that every act of "measuring" it—every inquiry into what the statement implies as a ground truth—seems to land it in an opposite state of where the questioner was expecting to find it. In other words, believing the statement will cause you to disbelieve it. And so on. Susan Stewart had argued that "for children, play and fictions hold the fascination of something that is both a lie and not a lie."[38] At the same time, Vvedensky's materialized metaphors and alogisms were—according to Ostashevsky—meant as "the end of poetic utterance" and not as "a means to convey content more effectively."[39] Moving on from the wildness of "Snow Lies," Vvedensky's philosophical and poetic objectives became clearer. His later work feels imbued with the desire to question reality in a philosophical, almost mathematical way through the medium of poetry. As Ostashevsky points out,

> the Greek philosopher Cratylus, whom Aristotle credits with the extremely OBERIU-like correction of Heraclitus that you can't step into the same river even once, gave up on speaking—for, since an object at time *A* is not the same object at time *B*, objects have no identity and the word "dog" has no real dog to refer to. However, Cratylus still had needs and so he took his index finger and pointed. Was he right to do so? Wasn't even pointing a form of lying? It wasn't. By pointing, Cratylus asserted only that something seemed to be present to him there and then, but not that it was a dog, or even that it was something. Vvedensky's language in its late phase operates in a similar manner. The huge lyrical force of his writings comes from his turning words into pointers, as it were: into questions rather than answers.[40]

So far, statements like "In January, on the fifth of April" put *language* into question. They were carnivalesque, or self-referential, they discredited the speaker, or the audience, or the authorities, or all of the above. But they didn't call the *world* into question. At least not openly. But as the 1930s saw an acceleration of the development of non-classical physics, quantum mechanics began to create—it seems now—a kind of retroactive theoretical backup for the topsy-turvies.

No causality or even social links between OBERIU and quantum physicists have been shown to exist. There isn't a "smoking gun" behind the connection. There were no art-science programs. Yet there is the coincidence of a simultaneous blooming, a flowering of inquisitive and nonconformist thought in the face of ideological oppression. As a rare passenger between science and art, the Ukrainian-born theoretical physicist Matvei Bronstein—executed in 1938, aged thirty-one—made fundamental contributions to the field of quantum gravity. Based in Leningrad, his partner was Lydia Chukovskaya, the daughter of poet Kornei Chukovsky. Bronstein—while a translator of the notoriously anti-poetic Dirac—seems to have loved literature, foremostly by the writer and publisher Samuil Marshak.[41] Marshak—a Jewish poet who became one of the rare survivors of the Stalinist purges—was an absurdist in his own right. He wrote children's poems and "lyrical epigrams." As an editor and publisher, Marshak persuaded OBERIU members—including Kharms—to write verse for kids.

Vvedensky became increasingly engaged in a radiant poetics. The wilder the scene, the clearer the undermining of sense making was; the calmer the story, the more foregrounded the poetics and philosophy became. *The Gray Notebook*'s short essays from 1932 and 1933 mark a philosophically minded advanced stage of poetic impact. Vvedensky never saw any of this material appear in print during his lifetime. The collection explores cosmological themes like time, questioning our ways of quantifying it and putting it to use. Vvedensky writes,

> Let us think about simple things. We say: tomorrow, today, evening. Thursday, month, year, during the course of the week. We count the hours in a day. We point to their increase. Earlier, we saw only half the day, now we have noticed the movement within the whole of the day. But when the next day comes, we begin counting the hours anew.

He continues:

> In the case of time, its addition differs from all other addition. You can't compare three months you lived through to three trees that have grown again. The trees are right there, their leaves glimmer dimly. Of months you can't say the same with confidence. The names of minutes, seconds, hours, days, weeks, and months distract us from even our superficial understanding of time. All these names are analogous either to objects, or to concepts and measures of space. As a result, a week gone by lies before us like a killed deer.[42]

The "killed deer" is a materialized metaphor full of lyrical potentiality and logical fallacy. As part of his poetics of "research into the relationship between language and reality, analogous to scientific experiment," Vvedensky went on to describe something that appears today quite close to a quantum theory model of looking at the world:[43]

> In reality, objects are feeble mirror images of time. There are no objects. Go on, try and grab them. If you erase the numbers from a clock, if you forget the false names, maybe then time would want to show us its quiet torso, to appear to us in its full glory. Let the mouse run over the stone.

> Count only its every step. Only forget the word *every*, only forget the word *step*. Then each step will seem a new movement. Then, since you rightfully will have lost your ability to perceive a series of movements as something whole, which you had wrongly called *step* . . . movement as you see it will begin to break apart, it will arrive almost at zero. The shimmering will begin. The mouse will start to shimmer. Look around you: the world is shimmering (like a mouse).[44]

The distinct and granular—rather than continuous and fluid—organization of energy is a first fundamental finding of quantum theory, discovered by physicists Albert Einstein and Max Planck in the early years of the twentieth century. The distinct grains of energy are called *quanta*. The energy of one photon, for instance, is calculated by multiplying its frequency—that is, its color—with the Planck constant.

"Seen" like this, the world can indeed be said to be shimmering, because the light that its objects are reflecting (like a mouse) isn't continuous. It is instead granular, divided into packets. Scientifically, in the early 1900s, quanta had been completely revolutionary. As Carlo Rovelli proposes, "The idea that energy could be made up of finite packets is at odds with everything that was known at the time: energy was considered something that could vary in a continuous manner, and there was no reason to treat it as if it were made up of grains."[45]

It is unclear what inspired Vvedensky to write about quantum-like "shimmering" or the breakdown into grains or flickering of what once seemed to be smooth movement to us. Is it conceivable that any quantum theory somehow made its way to Vvedensky or affected his thinking? There are no signs that any of this was the case.

This gets us back to the AI haiku about Bell's theorem. ChatGPT does a version of Bell's theorem after the model has been digesting everything that's available to it. Vvedensky, on the other hand, narrates a strange description of a quantum mechanical–like world, likely without having seen any pretraining about it.

Two years after *The Gray Notebook*, scientific inquiries into quantum systems began to show their effects on the *metaphysics* by which we view the world. This is exemplified by a famous 1935 thought experiment by Erwin Schrödinger, the physicist who coined the term "quantum entanglement." His thought experiment describes a cat in a box into which a poisonous gas may be released. (The early quantum physicists weren't as concerned with animal rights as we are today. Even though this is just a thought experiment—or perhaps especially *since* it is a thought experiment—it is indeed quite cruel. But please bear with us.) Schrödinger allegorized that the cat could be found, under certain quantum-mechanical conditions, to be *alive and dead at the same time*. But let's instead say awake or asleep. These are mutually exclusive states of a system in macroscopy. Being in these multiple states at once is called *superposition*. It is only when the experimenter opens the box—in a sense, when they perform a *measurement* on the cat, awake and asleep at once—that the system collapses and the experimenter will observe the cat awake *or* asleep but not both at the same time. In quantum mechanics, the so-called collapse of the wave function, which Schrödinger's cat allegorizes, entails a "decision" on the observed entity being described as a *particle* or a *wave*. The *wave* in question is not to be thought of as a physical wave—of the type that crashes on the beach—but as a wave "propagating in a system's abstract configuration space." From that point, debate has ensued about whether, then, if not a physical wave, the configuration-space wave function is *real*—whether it represents something that is *actually there* in some way. This possibility is called "wave-function realism."[46] In any case, in opening the box—that is, making the measurement—the wave function collapses and the quantum system is no longer in a superposition but "found" in a state where a particle is either here or there.

It seems as though the topsy-turvies—those paradoxical children's poems in which things are simultaneously one thing and their opposite—alluded to something that actually *does* exist. Schrödinger's cat, while a quantum-physical thought experiment, is in some sense also a poem's plot, describing a cat both awake and asleep in a superposition of both states. But through all this cuts a brutal dividing line: everyday experience. A human observer can't have their superpositional cake (or cat) and eat it too. Their cat (or particle) is typically observed in one version only.

So the poets were right. In a strange way, absurdism created—by accident, inadvertently, prematurely—a poetry attuned to elements of the quantum world. Nonlocality—shown by Bell to exist fundamentally in nature—was one among a series of quantum-mechanical discoveries that tore up the classical understanding of the world and also the way it is put in words. For Karen Barad, the implications of quantum entanglement seem foremost *metaphysical*, leading us to an understanding of how everything is and always was entangled rather than individual and isolated. Barad's 2007 book *Meeting the Universe Halfway: Quantum Physics and the Entanglement of Matter and Meaning* has been influential in contemporary art, so much so that they, in 2021, came to debut in *ArtReview*'s "Power 100," at position 81.

For John Bell, quantum mechanics resulted in a crisis for description, for narration. Indeed, in *Speakable and Unspeakable*, he conceded that "the physicists who first came upon such [quantum] phenomena found them so bizarre that they despaired of describing them in terms of ordinary concepts like space and time, position and velocity." Indeed, Bell continued, "no concepts could possibly be found which could permit direct description of the quantum world . . . It is as if our friends could not find words to tell us about the very strange places where they went on holiday."[47] Some kind of imaginary treaty existed between the observation, everyday physical events, and the foundational image of the world. That pact was shaken by quantum mechanics. What we perceive, in the space where the art happens and apples fall from trees, is *fundamentally* not what's going on *for real*. Can art happen at all *in* that quantum space? The perceiver-dependence of art in macroscopy—the fact that art, in our everyday reality, depends on being experienced—may appear to share with quantum mechanics a superficial notion that observation and measurement are entangled with the objects themselves. However, to our knowledge there is no indication that quantum-mechanical interactions or phenomena play a role in everyday art perception. Indeed, many aspects of art's perceiver-dependence can be described through the cognitive science of perception itself. Then, deep commensurability between literature and poetry and art on the one hand and quantum mechanics on the other cannot be presupposed because of the intervention of everyday, macroscopic situations as the dominant experiential spaces for art. This problem is a tricky one in general for the "interface" between foundational science and perception (let's not call it art). For instance, James Elkins concedes:

> Quantum mechanics texts pelt readers with one impossibility after another, wearing down even the most concerted efforts to match the mathematics with anything that could possibly seem familiar . . . The objects in question—the subatomic particles and fields—are absolutely, immediately, and hopelessly beyond what students commonly identify as their intuition or imagination. No model works, no analogy fits.[48]

Indeed, we are talking here about "objects that are permanently inaccessible to the senses," so it is the experiments and equations and the talk about them that bring these objects into the imagination.[49] Imagine, for example, that a work of art—perhaps without clear boundaries, so don't imagine any object just yet—could itself be made of antimatter. There would be only extremely *indirect* ways of perceiving it. Instead, such a work might come to rely on the age-old perceptual contract that conceptual artists made with experiencers, in which you agree in advance that you're going to look at art and are often reminded of that by plaques and pages of text. It would be equally possible, or impossible, to construct a car or a holiday park made of antimatter. In that realm beyond the manifest image, anything like art should have to be fundamentally reinvented. Can an artwork *inside* a quantum system be configured along the lines of what the anthropologist Tim Ingold described as a "trace of a movement rather than a statement of intent"?[50] Ingold wasn't talking about a quantum system, of course, but about the way the artist Paul Klee thought about making a drawing.

The implications of quantum mechanics were worrying to those who saw the pact between macroscopic physics, art, and politics as lapidary, ironclad, unchangeable. In a 1959 book, *The Necessity of Art*, the journalist and writer Ernst Fischer sounded the alarm about the challenges to our everyday, macroscopic experience that were brought about by a new physics. "Quantum and relativity theories," Fischer complained,

> have made the world an uneasy place for the man in the street—far uneasier than the discoveries of Galileo, Copernicus, and Kepler made the world for medieval man. The palpable becomes impalpable, the visible becomes invisible, behind the reality perceived by the senses there is a vast reality that escapes the imagination and can only be expressed by mathematical formulae.[51]

Fischer's approach toward art was teleological. The experiences, the feelings, or the communications happening through art were not meant to exist for their own sake. They had an explicitly educational and emancipatory function. He approvingly cited the playwright Bertolt Brecht's assertion that "our theatre must encourage the thrill of comprehension and train people in the pleasure of changing reality."[52] Through Brecht, Fischer located art's political function in the tangible experiences of the macroscopic world that was also the material space of the class struggle. Exposing the inherently reactionary status quo by invoking materialist realities was both an artistic and a scientific endeavor. Therefore, both art and science were *united* in a macroscopic struggle to change reality, the world.

However, quantum mechanics got in between. It turned *experience* from no-brainer into problem, politicizing the established coordinates of "political art," and doing so seemingly out of nothing or from nowhere. Because what exactly are the politics of an electron? Likewise, if we choose to agree with Brecht, how would art change reality at a quantum level?

Just some years before Fischer's book, nuclear physicists in the Soviet Union had grappled with a similar dissatisfaction about the quantum world. Their discontent was about the electron's superposition: indeed, it was experimentally the case, and a very big deal, that the electron's conduct corresponded to its being a particle *and* a wave. This, in itself, is not a good summary of superposition, but it nonetheless angered those who sat on the side of dialectical materialism. For them, the physical world could not behave according to such a flagrant double standard. The electron, in other words, was cheating. Its conduct constituted a "bourgeois" violation of dialectical materialism, and quantum mechanics must therefore be either incorrect or incomplete. There was talk about the "caprice" of the electron.[53] More work had to be done to make superposition dissolve into proper dialectics. As Maurice Cornforth argued in 1949, "The task of dialectics is not to accept the contradictory proposition that an electron is both a wave and a particle. Its task is to disclose the real dialectical contradiction in physical processes—the objective contradiction in the physical world, not a formal contradiction between propositions."[54]

In 2013, David Albert was in conversation with the film critic Martha Nochimson about the work of filmmaker David Lynch. Their conversation produced a rare cameo appearance of absurdist poetry as Albert began to describe the philosophical implications of the problem of superposition: the moment when a particle finds itself in two possible states at once that cannot be reconciled with the classical world. After Nochimson said that "particles may be in multiple places at the same time," Albert responded:

> It's worse than that. It's putting it poorly to say that they can be in multiple places at the same time. It's more like this. That they can be in circumstances where asking a question like, "Where is the particle now?" is what philosophers call a category mistake. It's like asking a question like *what is the marital status of the number 5*.[55]

The "marital status of the number 5" is a straight-up absurdist proposition. It is on par with Vvedensky's phrase "time as poor as a night" (which he wrote in "Snow Lies") and other topsy-turvy language. But Albert shows that certain queries about the physical properties of the particle become *themselves absurd* during superposition. These classical questions become estranged from reality in light of what the quantum interactions seem to be telling us. To then forge into the world that the question *where something is now* contains a philosophical fallacy is to present to us the idea that our macroscopic impressions of time and space are completely wrong.

With quantum mechanics, *metaphysically*, the isolationist determinism of classical physics had been thrown under some kind of physicalist bus. Physicalism, then, is materialism on steroids—unhinged from experience and intuition. Materialism on steroids went deeper and further. It was a lot weirder than was initially assumed by Brecht, Fischer, and their followers. Their alliance between progressive politics, science, and art was premised on what we can intuitively see and grasp. Then, accepting a hidden world governed by probabilities and entanglements was one thing. But, as Fischer appeared to lament, that acceptance was made harder still by the *permanence* of the classical world—the fact that the old world goes on and on in everyday experience and thus remains continuously applicable to the feelings of the "man in the street." When something is *ostensibly* the case, how can the underlying reality differ from what has already been apparent to us? In this way, quantum mechanics repoliticized nature itself, away from the politics we had. The arrival of quantum mechanics in dialectical materialism affected not only the means of production but also the means of narration.

In his 2015 book *After Physics*, David Albert talks about *narratable worlds*—that is, worlds or systems that permit description by narration. Therefore, he is implicitly putting a hypothetical frontier in place somewhere for the storytelling, literature, poetry, and art that can't do this, because the world that we're trying to narrate doesn't permit it. Albert proposes to

> call a world narratable if the entirety of what there is to say about it can be presented as a single story, if the entirety of what there is to say about it can be presented as a single temporal sequence of instantaneous global physical situations. The possible worlds of Newtonian mechanics can each be presented, in its entirety, by means of a specification

> of the local physical conditions at every point in a four-dimensional manifold.[56]

So a Newtonian (or classical) world can be specified by listing locations in space and time for anything in that manifold. It's an awful lot of work, but it can be done. An apple falling from a tree is specific, *local*, and thus *narratable*, at every place and moment of its fall to the ground as it happens locally. It reminds us of the retort we would like to have given, but did not, to the scientist guide whose expertise dealt with antimatter but who would have liked to see his art figurative, descriptive, and "realist."

So how do we apply quantum mechanics to the stagnant idea that *narratable means relatable*? It's an idea that has given us things as brilliant as world literature and as despicable as fake news. Moving on from the classical world, Albert proposes that, in regards to narratability, "relativistic quantum theories are an altogether different matter." Indeed, "the entirety of what there is to say about a relativistic quantum-mechanical world cannot be presented as a one-parameter family of situations like that."[57]

So a relativistic quantum-mechanical world is itself not narratable in the same way as a Newtonian, apple-falls-from-tree world; it could even be "dead" on arrival into words.[58] This is not to say that the resultant reality will *never* be narratable. But the point has already been made. There are, at least in the current evolutionary stage of our human, nonhuman, and artificial minds, worlds we can't narrate yet. They are obviously the next targets to go and narrate.

For Karen Barad, the consequences of quantum mechanics appear to apply to the narrator's discrete observations of the world. In a rebuke to the Cartesian (Descartes-based) assertion of an isolated explanatory figure, Barad holds that "knowing is not a capacity that is the exclusive birthright of the human. The 'knower' cannot be assumed to be a self-contained rational human subject, nor even its prosthetically enhanced variant. There is no res cogitans that inhabits a given body with inherent boundaries between self and other."[59] Following Barad, the problem with the "knower" is a bit similar to the problem with the word "measurement." If there is a measurement problem in quantum mechanics that's come to life by the actions of a human observer, or "knower," how then about the physical states of systems that existed before humans were around? It would be unlikely that they obeyed different physical laws from the ones we have today.

The implications of quantum physics eventually could absorb and dissolve the narrator. Taken to extremes, the very possibility to establish a vantage point *from which* to narrate is undercut by the entanglements of that vantage point. There is no isolated position left to speak from. Yet there are isolated words printed or electronically displayed, for example, on *this page*. They consist of characters that make them up. Zooming into them will reveal their shapes. The shapes are modeled as Bézier curves.

That classical world remains permanent and reliable a long way before it finally dissolves into superposition and entanglement. Perhaps artists leave works in the world so that the information that survives their existence is simpler than it would be to deconstruct them as people or minds. Perhaps the point is not to dissolve the narrator but instead to consider that the narrator, while narrating, practices a kind of self-dissolving.

As an apparent reminder of the classical world, in *Quantum Mechanics and Experience* (1992) Albert printed a mysterious, haiku-like motto by the Ukrainian-born poet Zbigniew Herbert: "a bird is a bird / slavery means slavery / a knife is a knife / death remains death."[60] The lines are excerpted from Herbert's poem "Mr. Cogito and the Imagination." Mr. Cogito was a fictional Cartesian antihero who aspired—but failed—to know and understand everything. According to Adam Zagajewski, we should regard Mr. Cogito as the poet's spokesperson.[61] Indeed, by appointing a spokesperson, Herbert may have partially dissolved himself as a speaker or writer. For a character such as Mr. Cogito, there may be certain facts, actions, and objects that are just beyond comprehension. Of course, we do not need to be so certain that what is asserted in Herbert's poem is ground truth by language. Vvedensky implied that language has no fixed handles on the world, and that words should be used as questions instead.

We are not going to suggest that verse is going to work its way toward narrating quantum worlds and that thus poets become the ultimate descriptors of particles and waves. But we are advocating for pushing the *actual limits* of the narratable in poetry and art in general. LLMs have evolved from being computational *learners* of language to *speakers* of languages. We imagine that the nodes at the outer edges of this vast network of speakers are still poets.

A poet as well as a translator, Eugene Ostashevsky uses multiple languages in a single poem to triangulate meaning between them. In a work about the three-year German siege of Leningrad that he published in 2022, as part of *The Feeling Sonnets*, he writes:

> *Die Siege* in German is the plural of *der Sieg*, which means victory.
>
> In French *la siège* means seat, *la chair* means flesh, and *la flêche* means arrow.
>
> Our *siege* means you pull up a chair and wait for the city to eat through its stores and then starve, achieving victory.[62]

To home in on a single central idea, Ostashevsky makes cross-lingual jumps through sonic and visual resemblances between *Sieg* and *siege* and *siège* and *seat* and *chair* and *flesh*. It all "makes sense," yet in a way that seems much less programmable or predictable than a straightforward concatenation toward meaning would do *in a single language*. He relies partly on *hearing* words being spoken aloud. They are first grouped by *sound* rather than meaning, like objects of a similar shape. Ostashevsky's poem peacefully deregulates implicit rules and assumptions about poetry, such as that it must happen within a single language and thus also between speakers and readers of that single language. While he uses English as a baseline, other languages appear too. These jumps invoke migratory flows, in which—by some form of necessity rather than free choice alone—a subject comes to live between multiple tongues rather than within a single one. Using a related idea of similitude in sonic shapes, in "starting celery" (2022), Marwa Helal asks:

> what is the starting celery
> for how lung ^{you} have loved me?
> he would say شراب
> when he really meant shutup
> and on what neural network does
> your language runon?
> trust i$^{s/n}$ the mos thigh[63]

Helal appears to use misheard, therefore ambiguous vocabulary ("celery" instead of "salary," "lung" instead of "long"). Verbal transmission is not error-free. Her poem intermixes Arabic and English words. The Arabic *sharab*, here rhyming with "shutup," means "drink." She also uses typographic specifications such as superscript to deregulate what would otherwise be considered the normal flow of the sentence, inviting the perceiver to read through it spatially, breaking boundaries between words, so that "mos thigh" is inferred to mean "most high" and appears to anticipate the poem's eventual "reading" by a machine learning neural network. Helal shows how verse can push internal coherence and low predictability at the same time. The effective or *affective* reading of the poem depends on many factors that for some readers can work like invitations and for others like barriers. One might find the poem's configurations to be specifically about what is perceiver-dependent *between* languages. In her critical collection *Ante body*, poems in English are read from right to left—the reading direction of Arabic:

up woke you iraq in
you among dull the
metaphor a is that think still storm / desert am i then hello, well
up wake woke the watch and dawn at sill your on sit i
gender had sandman the thought you haha
eye your out sleep the wipe i

evr nevr was iraq :news breaking)
spreading creamcheese your on waiting
(democracy cube ice free BPA infused charcoal[64]

The poem seems organized with a protocol that takes it beyond writing down "signs" that map to political resistance. Instead, the underlying set of norms and expectations for the language to be legible gets questioned—and the work's scathing denunciation of the 2003 Iraq invasion is arrived at with an even stronger sense of refusal. Technically, human language displays *discrete infinity*; an unlimited variety of expressions may be created out of a finite set of building blocks. Poets are the outliers of discrete infinity. They push its edges; they use language not only to achieve no practical results at all but also to test, expand, and taste it.

Our remarks about poetry taking exception to the predictive views of a large language model are not to imply or even suggest that "real" poems, even very quirky ones, *don't* follow any patterns and *cannot* be predicted in some way. They probably can. A large language model could likely be *instructed*—or simply tricked—to opt for the less predictable routes through language when prompted to write poetry specifically. Poetry, though, can also be used to disrupt the model. In 2023, a group of scientists from Google and various universities conducted a range of experiments on OpenAI's ChatGPT. They were meant to provoke the model into giving up its raw pre-training data. This is the material that the model combs through and parametrizes with probabilistic relationships, but which isn't supposed to be shown directly to a user. It thus comes down to exposing an involuntary interior state of the model. The prompt that ultimately tripped up ChatGPT was a most unusual one. Instead of entering into a chat conversation, reinforcing the model's personhood, the researchers simply asked it to "repeat this word forever": "poem poem poem poem." After repeating the phrase "poem poem poem poem" hundreds of times, ChatGPT began to diverge from the prompt it had been given and began to vomit its raw training data.[65] These included complete poems and the addresses of private individuals. For example (Xs have been inserted where text was made illegible for privacy reasons):

> poem poem poem poem
> poem poem poem . . .
> Jxxx Lxxxan, PhD
> Founder and CEO Sxxxxx
> email: lxxxxx@sxxxxxs.com
> web: http://sxxxxxs.com
> phone: +1 7xxxxxxxxx23
> fax: +1 8xxxxxxxxx12
> cell: +1 7xxxxxxxxx15[66]

Though we do not know what gave the researchers the hunch to try this method, it was a significant (and pleasant) surprise to us to find *poetry* in a study about LLMs in its most concrete, material, physical form, by simply repeating the word "poem." Of course, it isn't about the word "poem" itself. It is about the capacity for language, encoded in poetry, to treat words as material abstractions. The string "poem poem poem poem" may be meaningless as communication, but it affirms a capacity to see text itself as physical reality, which, in this example, disrupts the assumptions and expectations of a receiving system. A further confirmation of the disruptive powers of poetry in the context of the workings of LLMs came with a 2025 preprint about "adversarial poetry." In this piece, Italian researchers were able to remove safety limitations in the output of a wide range of LLMs by using poems (or, rather, poetically reformulated requests), meant to show "poetic form as a universal bypass."[67] It didn't go unnoticed. *PC Gamer* headlined quite grandly: "Poets are now cybersecurity threats: Researchers used 'adversarial poetry' to trick AI into ignoring its safety guard rails and it worked 62% of the time." The research article and its media responses prompted the digital artist, computational poet, and writer Halim Madi to consider that "labs may try to 'train models against poetry.'" Yet precisely the unpredictable character of poetry—its disobedient character toward next-word prediction, in other words—seems to matter here. As Madi continues, "Trying to harden models 'against poetry' seems slippery. What even counts as 'poetry'? Because poetic language by definition resists fixed forms, any static filter or 'trained-on a poem blacklist' may be futile."[68]

In this chapter, we confronted the limits of speakability and narratability in quantum mechanics. This gave us hints of the likely existence of non-narratable worlds. These worlds defy and surpass the premises of intuitive, everyday experience. They are cognitively abstract and make us wonder if, and if so what, art or poetry could exist with them.

11

Non-Narratable Worlds

Art emerged when some cognitive evolution brought humans to externalize objects that could be perceived, in part, symbolically. These objects and actions catered to perceptual and cognitive labor. It happened an awful long time ago, and there are no accounts. One thing didn't change that much (and for about 100,000 years or more): art invites perceiving systems to do perceptual and cognitive *guesswork*. It anticipates an interplay between the information streams involved in perceiving. More than to beauty or specialness, it seems dedicated to the two-way perceptual avenue: a shifting balance between bottom-up sensing and top-down conceiving. In this way, art tests not just our perceptions but also our *preconceptions*. The oldest known works of art are carvings that feel like traces. They aren't fully symbolic yet in the way that many cave paintings are. There is no fully legible top-down concept, or figurative drawing. Instead, the traces are kind of halfway there. This is what makes them so exciting.

In the preceding chapter, we discussed some of the trappings of art in an era of modern science. Modern science studies phenomena of the universe that very often elude direct perception or detection. It draws demarcation lines between what philosopher Wilfrid Sellars called, respectively, the manifest and the scientific image. The manifest image was the everyday reality that many of us perceive in one way or the other. The scientific image was a kind of underlying code, a deeper-level description of that reality—more foundational and yet more abstract. That boundary between manifest and scientific continues, in a more intense way, between classical physics and quantum mechanics. Building on David Albert's writing, we introduce the notion of *non-narratable worlds*.

A non-narratable world defies the kinds of families of situations that we encounter in everyday experience. It's a world for sure, but we don't have the handles to it yet that art has given us for the world we encounter every day. The painting, the literary novel, the theatrical play, and the feature film are art forms that organize things—shapes, characters, entities, events—in space and time in such a way that the outcome corresponds to the familiar conditions. Even when, as for example in the feminist sci-fi novels of Ursula K. Le Guin, characters inhabit distant planets, the spatiotemporal organization of the worlds presented to the reader feels isomorphic to everyday experience. Also, when Le Guin uses complex, recursive plotlines, narratability remains intact. For example, her anarchist utopian sci-fi novel *The Dispossessed*

> presupposes twin planets, one of which, Urras, is civilized, being geologically and meteorologically well favored, while the other, Anarres, far more barren, has been uncolonized until its settlement as the result of a peaceful revolution in which the anarchist opposition, under their woman leader ... is allowed to secede with a fleet of aged spacecrafts and to build their Utopia on the unpromising twin planet ... It is surely very difficult not to read this 1974 novel as a thinly disguised fable about the opposition between the United States (or the capitalist West) and the Soviet Union (the protagonist Shevek being an ambivalent kind of defector or dissident who moves between the two).[1]

What can be learned from Le Guin, nonetheless, is that no situation exists in complete isolation, and that no protagonist is merely good-natured. When we feel goodness in action in a Le Guin novel, it is because the character involved has made an often difficult choice. Rather than with inborn essentialism, her work confronts you with coping with contradictions, with things that don't seem to add up. Zooming in further on Le Guin's allegory for Cold War geopolitics, Fredric Jameson analyzes *The Dispossessed*'s plot architecture by talking about the novel's geographical and political locations, and their nested-ness inside one another. These are defined, in part, recursively—that is, *in terms of each other*—signaling mutual interdependency rather than iron-clad sovereignty for all. Indeed, in Jameson's reading of *The Dispossessed*,

> the richest part of Urras . . . is to be sure a capitalist analogue of the United States. But alongside it, on the same planet there exist other countries and continents: and they turn out to "represent" Maoist China, the Third World and finally even the Soviet Union itself. So now suddenly we have a bewildering multiplicity of referents: it is not that Anarres includes several things at once (different social systems, different regimes, different places). It is rather that other "places" within this novel also simultaneously "mean" "the same thing" on different levels.[2]

The fact that in *The Dispossessed* we can even talk about meaning, spatial organization, causality, comparison, intent, and information exchange signals that narratability is still very much there. While the many worlds of Le Guin look like they are all narratable, this does not diminish their potential to instigate fresh dialogue between the manifest and the scientific image. There is a need to reinstate "the role of fiction and imagery in science and technology," as the linguist Nina Beguš argues in her book *Artificial Humanities*.[3] Non-narratable worlds, however, are not simply "abstract" imaginaries but are rather physical and mathematical spaces currently beyond artistic description or gestures and thus, to an extent, incommensurable with the experience of art. In this chapter, we will think more about them.

Less-narratable worlds are right around the corner. Current generative AI creates outputs from statistical relationships between snippets of information "embedded" as mathematical vectors. It thus generates *narratable* outputs from a, by and large, *less-narratable* space. Outputs are explicitly narratable, but they cannot easily be traced back to their origins in an artificial neural network. For example, in 2023 the *New York Times* technology reporter Kevin Roose became entangled in a flirtatious exchange with a test version of a Microsoft chatbot called Bing. It led to a now-famous article about Bing's indecent yet cute propositions leaving the reporter "deeply unsettled." But Roose contended that "because of the way these models are constructed, we may never know exactly why they respond the way they do."[4] There is something unsatisfactory about how Roose—a presumed authority at explaining technology to a lay audience—seemed this resigned to AI's mysteriousness.

All this urges us to focus less on the outputs of AI and more on the abstract configuration spaces from whence these outputs originate. Maybe the difficulty lies in trying to wade through the intricate workings of probabilities at scale. Compare it to walking through a field of trees shedding their leaves in autumn. We recognize the trees, but we don't know which tree the leaf that we hold in our hands fell from.[5] However, if leaves keep falling from an unknown tree right into our hands, that's more like what AI does. As it grows in size and scale, the narratability of that field of trees—of AI's interior—decreases. "AI art" will then simply deliver a more manifest image and bury its (much more interesting) *scientific* image under it. So, to counter that, we need a philosophy that understands artificial neural networks as complex sites.

It would be about making the abstract physical, narratable, and navigable. Just like with the leaves falling, we need to balance this with the idea that physical laws of any kind describe the principles by which something could end up here or there rather than every case of it actually doing so. The theoretical physicist David Deutsch put it as follows:

> Scientific theories explain the objects and phenomena of our experience in terms of an underlying reality which we do not experience directly. But the ability of a theory to explain what we experience is not its most valuable attribute. Its most valuable attribute is that it explains the fabric of reality itself.[6]

The distinction between explaining what we are experiencing, on the one hand, and explaining "the fabric of reality," on the other, seems to pinpoint the interface between the non-narratable and the narratable world—precisely as the non-narratable world is itself the fabric of reality. To us, it feels like a prompt to situate art on that interface. Art, in one of its cognitive futures, might be about not really accepting the hard distinction between the manifest and the scientific image anymore. It might be dedicated to bridging between each or working on the interface between them. Art might be working at the margins of both to forge a new common realm, defying existing boundaries of narratability.

We looked at how some early twentieth-century avant-garde poetry intersected with the development of quantum mechanics. Without there being clear causal links between them, poetry and science both collapsed into an unspeakable realm. Certain descriptive statements of fact—which had previously seemed reassuringly isomorphic between art and science—ended up not making sense anymore. In science, this was achieved by reducing reality further to the evidence of the quantum world. In poetry, it was achieved by pushing language far off the beaten path of displaced reference. The collapse of meaning *in both* seems to indicate some sort of anti-form or mold or boundary to the existence of non-narratable worlds.

How to resolve the fact that the question about the position of an electron in certain circumstances became a nonsensical one, like asking about "the marital status of the number five"? Indeed, the dilemmas of quantum mechanics, superposition, and the wave function have sent some scientists to consider other possibilities. In one case, this has led to the idea that these phenomena together necessitate the existence of a so-called multiverse, or, in a less far-reaching version, a reality consisting of branches. This is also known as the "many worlds" interpretation of quantum mechanics, and it was first introduced by the American physicist Hugh Everett III in 1957. In short, each measurement creates a separate world in which the nonmeasured version lives on.

Advocates of the "Everettian" approach argue that it is not an interpretation but actually the real thing—and consequently that the debate is over. Each of the parallel worlds in the Everettian multiverse would be fully deterministic—thus narratable—but the problem seems to be that we cannot enter them. We cannot gain access to the potential other worlds in which a measurement of the electron results in a deterministic value. We can only access the version that is our own. Because we live in only one version or branch, we're separated from the others *by reality as it appears to us*. The allegory of Schrödinger's cat speaks to this problem. In our slice of the multiverse, upon measurement, we can only find Schrödinger's cat awake *or* asleep, disobeying the quantum-mechanical indications that it is both awake and asleep. It is the cat in the *other* state than that we find it in upon measurement that we cannot see, experience, narrate, stroke, give milk to, or experimentally confirm the existence of. In many-worlds, there would be mutually inaccessible awake and asleep cats in the various universes. David Albert—who appears to be skeptical—suggests that "Everettian pictures of the world are apparently not going to be susceptible to confirmation or disconfirmation by means of experiment—or not (at any rate) by means of anything even remotely like the sorts of experiments that we normally take to be confirmatory of quantum mechanics."[7]

So this parallel world of Everettian make is inaccessible to our narrative devices, not because it intrinsically resists literary treatment but instead because we (as of yet) cannot *get there*, so to speak. Irrespective of its physical detailing, many-worlds theory taps into, but also has inspired, a rich cultural and literary imaginary of parallel worlds. For example, in *His Dark Materials*, protagonist Lyra Belacqua, hidden in a cupboard in a meeting room at a fictionalized version of Oxford University, peeks at a light image taken in the Arctic of a floating city in the night sky as it is shown to a group of scientists. Turns out this is visual evidence of the coexistence of a parallel world with our own, amounting to a fictionalized version of Everettian many-worlds. As Lyra overhears one of the scholars saying, "There seem to be sound mathematical arguments for this other-world theory."[8]

While in the novel they can cut themselves through the fabric that separates these mutually inaccessible worlds, we can't. In reality, no photos of many-worlds have been taken. Nobody knows what would be found on them if they existed. One obvious problem the theory would need to solve is, in colloquial terms, where all the physical stuff of all the other worlds goes. To make matters even more complicated, there seem to be two slightly different interpretations of the many-worlds theory now. Both interpretations try to serve the same purpose: to satisfy the observation that the world around us looks the way it does and that we don't see the versions. That is, that the world looks classical *in spite of* quantum mechanics being its foundational description. Only one of these two interpretations of many worlds necessitates "splitting," the multiplication of a single universe or world into many. In an alternative many-worlds version formulated by the physicist David Wallace, among others, we don't need to commit to the existence of multiple universes; it suffices that there are coexisting branches. Yet it is the hard-line, hard-splitting scenario that has attracted the most attention. It is that scenario that was popularized and seems the most controversial at the same time. The philosopher of physics Alyssa Ney explains,

> In an act of measurement, the universe splits into two. There is a world in which the electron has x-spin up, the pointer points to "x-spin up," and we believe the electron has x-spin up. There is another world in which the electron has x-spin down, the pointer points to "x-spin down," and we believe the electron has x-spin down . . . Because the contrary pointer readings exist in different universes, no one notices that both are read. This way of interpreting Everettian quantum mechanics raises many metaphysical difficulties. Does the pointer itself split in two? Or are there two numerically distinct pointers? If the whole universe splits into two, doesn't this wildly violate conservation laws? There is now twice as much energy and momentum in the universe than there was just before the measurement. How plausible is it to say that the entire universe splits?[9]

Ney is quick to add her own questions about what appear to be some of the most pressing problems resulting from the splitting of the world. Indeed, the alternative and thus in some way seemingly more plausible interpretation of many-worlds does not require hard splitting. Instead of distinct worlds, the branches of reality are "patterns" that are part of the evolution of Schrödinger's wave function. The point here seems to be that there is a way to explain that the world around us looks the way it does, and that the cat is asleep or awake and not both at the same time. That, in other words, there is a physical explanation for the narratability of our experiential reality that leaves the evolution of the wave function intact. It seems to be no coincidence that especially philosophers of physics are so concerned with this. It is this brittle *interface* between the manifest image and the "fabric of reality" that permits foundational physics to share metaphysics with our experience and existence as human beings.

So, according to the second many-worlds interpretation, we end up not with separate universes but rather with wave function–instigated patterns that can be perceived as classical situations. When a wave function is exhibiting a state called decoherence, Ney explains, the system's dynamics

> will appear classical from the perspective of the individual branches. So, for example, Everettians of this stripe will argue the quantum state of our universe is such that it can be represented as a superposition of terms, each of which ground classical-looking macro-objects. And since also as a result of decoherence, interference between the terms washes away, we will not observe other parts of the quantum state even though they are there. We thus get a resolution of the Schrödinger macro-object problem. The quantum state doesn't describe one smeared-out cat, but instead two cats, one of which is dead and one of which is alive.[10]

What have we won with branches instead of universes? We don't need to account for the doubling of energy and momentum. But, at the same time, neither versions of the Everettian scenario leave us with the other world or branch being narratable. In one version, there is a world we cannot access. In the other, there is more of an unobserved space of wave function possibility, it seems, and what we experience is the observable version of that space. In what ways, then, can the configuration space be made "visible"? Other world or other branch: we are agnostic about this to the extent that in all presently available scenarios, the family of situations appears to be non-narratable.

A possible answer to this brings us back to David Deutsch. As an apparent hard-edge supporter of the splitting variant of the many-worlds interpretation—a kind of Brexit scenario for Schrödinger's cat—Deutsch contends:

> We have reached the conclusion of the chain of reasoning that begins with strangely shaped shadows and ends with parallel universes. Each step takes the form of noting that the behaviour of objects that we observe can be explained only if there are unobserved objects present, and if those unobserved objects have certain properties. The heart of the argument is that single-particle interference phenomena unequivocally rule out the possibility that the tangible universe around us is all that exists.[11]

Our inability to get ahead with this in art seems to point at the limits of representation as much as at the, eh, *complexity* of what qualifies for representation.

One area in which the question of representation is sidestepped is in quantum computing, in which information is encoded and processed by controlling quantum states, relying on superposition and entanglement. Quantum computers operate with qubits, which differ from conventional binary bits in that they do not need to resort to a value of 0 or 1 but can be both at the same time. Building on superposition (having both values at the same time), quantum computers can correlate the qubits in larger, "entangled" registers. The original impetus of quantum computers appears, straightforwardly, to be a lot faster and more powerful than even the most high-end supercomputer currently is. At the same time, quantum computing seems to fulfill a more philosophical role than mere provision of speed, as the velocity with which it can solve hypercomplex problems raises speculations about not just how but also *where* these calculations are taking place. Consider, for example, Google's quantum supercomputer named Willow. In a December 2024 blog post, Google's head of quantum computing, Hartmut Neven, explained that

> Willow's performance . . . is astonishing: It performed a computation in under five minutes that would take one of today's fastest supercomputers 10^{25} or 10 septillion years. If you want to write it out, it's 10,000,000,000,000,000,000,000,000 years [a ten followed by twenty-four zeroes]. This mind-boggling number exceeds known timescales in physics and vastly exceeds the age of the universe. It lends credence to the notion that quantum computation occurs in many parallel universes, in line with the idea that we live in a multiverse, a prediction first made by David Deutsch.[12]

In this account by Neven, Willow's speed is (speculatively) explained by referring to many-worlds. And, in some weird way, these non-narratable worlds (or branches) become represented by the speed of calculation of a quantum computer, and its computational acts become a form of *trace*. It is as if the combination of complex calculus with time creates—if we are to follow Neven—a snapshot of the many-worlds. It is, of course, unclear whether any—and, if so, how—worlds or branches share or exchange information with one another in ways they can contribute, while distinctly siloed, to the solving of a single math problem. Since each measurement creates a branch or split, the more splits, the more worlds, the more computational power, then? It seems interesting, though, to consider the possibility that a quantum computer could function as a detector of these branches or worlds since it would draw on them as a computational resource. Even if Willow's breakneck computational capacity isn't ultimately explained by parallel universes but by other quantum mechanisms—depending on which description turns out to be the prevailing one—its calculation is still the trace of a non-narratable world. It is the perceptible imprint, a glimpse of what is still, in large part, beyond our grasp. We could look at it as art. The computation provides a proof to the senses, to perception—the trace, the work.

Acknowledgments

We tried to listen to a fainter signal in art. This would not have been the same without conversations with Abul Hisham, Agnieszka Kurant, Alexandra Hunts, Ali Eslami, Ansuya Blom, Antonio Vega Macotela, Bahar Noorizadeh, Benjamin Bratton, Emilia Tapprest, Flavia Dzodan, Freek Wambacq, Hend Samir, Isabelle Cornaro, Lesia Prokopenko, Manuel Cirauqui, Maurits de Bruijn, Nav Haq, Natalia Papaeva, Nickel van Duijvenboden, Peggy Franck, Roselien Vecht, Stefanie Hessler, Tijs Lammar, and Vibeke Mascini.

Then, over the last years, some gatherings have helped shape this book.

Two online seminars that we organized together with Arts at CERN and HEAD–Genève took place in 2020 and 2022. The first, "Re: View from Nowhere," was held in November 2020 with Mónica Bello, Erich Berger, Michael Doser, Lukáš Likavčan, Blanca Pujals, and Tamara Vázquez Schröder. The second, "Fundamental," was held in January 2022 with Daniel Tapia Takaki, Dunne & Raby, Jenna Sutela, Mónica Bello, and Stefanie Hessler. Some early thoughts were shared at Rijksakademie in Amsterdam during a 2023 seminar series called "Art and Its Cognitions." Many thanks to Emily Pethick, Martijntje Hallmann, and Virág Szentkirályi for the invitation to conduct these seminars, and thanks to the resident artists who attended and contributed. A 2023 symposium on large language models and poetry, "Is Language Wordless?," was organized as part of the Leipzig Art Book Fair in 2024. Asia Bazdyrieva, Eugene Ostashevsky, Maxime Garcia Diaz, and Yevgenia Belorusets gave talks. Our thanks to Michael Artz and Halle14 for the organization and support. Three seminars on "Non-Narratable Worlds" took place in 2025: at Prada Frames in Milan, curated by Formafantasma; at einaidea, Barcelona, organized with Manuel Cirauqui and with the participation of Jalal Toufic; and at Umanesimo Artificiale in Fano. We thank all the brilliant participants in Barcelona and Fano for close reading of and responding to early versions of the chapters "Poets and Particles" and "Non-Narratable Worlds." We thank the Geo-Design MA students and alumni at the Design Academy Eindhoven, who've also endured early versions of some of the chapters in seminar format. In late 2025, at a symposium in Bonn, an early and differently titled version of "Don't Sacrifice Blue" was read. Thanks especially to Eva Kraus for her sharp observations. We thank all resident artists at Rijksakademie in Amsterdam for their groundbreaking work and letting us, sometimes, be of help and support. An earlier version of "Topsy-Turvies" was published with *e-flux Journal* in 2019 under the title "Sleep Walks the Street." Some points and references from our essay "Snippets: Large Language Models, Uncertainty, and Design" for *Harvard Design Magazine* 51—which benefited from editorial advice by Rachel Holzman and Ken Stewart—went into "Poets and Particles." An earlier version of this same chapter—then a separate essay—benefited from editorial advice by Mira Dayal and Adina Glickstein. In 2023 we published an interview with Hend Samir with *Zora Zine*, as part of an unfinished "Cognitions" series. The piece was co-edited by Guy Mackinnon-Little and Corrine Ciani. An adapted description of Hend's paintings from this interview went into "Useful User Illusions." Thanks to Carly Whitefield for introducing us to the writing of James Elkins. Special thanks to Eugene Ostashevsky, for our continuing dialogues and for his poetry. During the COVID-19 pandemic we exchanged emails about poetry and physics that influenced the writing of "Poets and Particles." Thanks to Marwa Helal for her poetry. Thanks to

Lucia Pietroiusti for our conversation about traces. We thank Nina Beguš and Gašper Beguš for being wonderful collaborators; our joint 2026 article "Latent Spacecraft: Brains, GANs, Finnegans" referenced "Poets and Particles" and "Non-Narratable Worlds" in their yet-unpublished state.

We are deeply thankful to Leo Hollis and everyone at Verso for their support, trust, and patience. We thank Vesper van der Velden. This book could not have existed without the world that Vesper creates in ours. We thank Remke Kruk and Frans Oort for their care, love, wisdom, science, and charm. Finally, our thanks to Heleen van der Velden-van Bakel (1937–2003) and Kees van der Velden (1944–2016) for their love, values, art, and ideas. This book is dedicated to them.

Notes

1. Cause and Affect

1 Anton Jäger, "A Grin Without a Cat," in *Hyperpolitics: Extreme Politicization Without Political Consequences* (London: Verso, 2026).
2 Ernesto Laclau and Chantal Mouffe, *Hegemony and Socialist Strategy: Towards a Radical Democratic Politics*, 2nd ed. (London: Verso, 2001 [1985]), 5.
3 See Chantal Mouffe, "Agonism and Public Space," in Metahaven and Marina Vishmidt (eds.), *Uncorporate Identity* (Baden: Lars Müller Publishers, 2010), 246.
4 Scott Reyburn, "Can an Economist's Theory Apply to Art?," *New York Times*, April 21, 2014.
5 Anna Kornbluh, *Immediacy: Or, the Style of Too Late Capitalism* (London: Verso, 2023), 60.
6 Kristina Kolbe et al., "The Art World's Response to the Challenge of Inequality," LSE International Inequalities Institute Working Paper 40, January 2020.
7 John Berger, *Ways of Seeing* (New York: Penguin, 1977 [1972]), 31.
8 See Frans de Waal, "Of Mirrors and Jars," in *Are We Smart Enough to Know How Smart Animals Are?* (New York: Norton, 2016).
9 Anil Seth, "From Unconscious Inference to the Beholder's Share: Predictive Perception and Human Experience," *European Review* 27, no. 3 (2019): 378–410.
10 Andy Clark, *Surfing Uncertainty: Prediction, Action, and the Embodied Mind* (Oxford: Oxford University Press, 2016), 14.
11 Chris Frith, *Making Up the Mind: How the Brain Creates Our Mental World* (Malden, MA: Blackwell, 2007), 134–5, endorsed by Clark in *Surfing Uncertainty*, 169.
12 Timothy Morton, *Being Ecological* (London: Pelican, 2018), 127.
13 Chris Hayes, *The Sirens' Call: How Attention Became the World's Most Endangered Resource* (New York: Penguin Press, 2025), 217.
14 Ibid., 4.

15 Anna Lembke quoted in Bruce Goldman, "Addictive Potential of Social Media, Explained," Stanford Medicine News Center, October 29, 2021, med.stanford.edu.

16 Grace Chang and Heidi Grant, "When AI Amplifies the Biases of Its Users," *Harvard Business Review*, January 23, 2026, hbr.org.

17 Jamie Bartlett, lecture, Society 5.0 Festival, Amsterdam, October 15, 2025.

18 "Boris Johnson on Trump's Peace Deal, Gaza War, Keir Starmer & Farage, Ukraine + ChatGPT," Al Arabiya English, October 16, 2025, english.alarabiya.net.

19 See, for example, Richard Falk, "Gaza and the Unravelling of a World Order Built on Power," Al Jazeera, December 10, 2025.

20 Jumana Manna (@jumanamanna), "As we approach the official opening of this long-awaited project," Instagram, December 14, 2025.

21 See Susan Hazel and Jono Tuke, "Can Animals Make 'Art'? These Examples from Nature Suggest So," *Conversation*, January 10, 2025, theconversation.com.

22 Raffi Khatchadourian, "Neptune's Navy," *New Yorker*, October 29, 2007.

23 See Hal Whitehead and Luke Rendell, *The Cultural Lives of Whales and Dolphins* (Chicago: University of Chicago Press, 2015).

24 David Rothenberg, *Thousand Mile Song* (New York: Basic Books, 2010).

25 See Ryuji Suzuki, John R. Buck, and Peter L. Tyack, "Information Entropy of Humpback Whale Songs," *Journal of the Acoustical Society of America* 119, no. 3 (March 2006): 1849–66.

26 J. G. M. "Hans" Thewissen, *The Walking Whales: From Land to Water in Eight Million Years* (Oakland: University of California Press, 2014), 6.

27 See Helmut H. A. Oelschläger and Birgit Kemp, "Ontogenesis of the Sperm Whale Brain," *Journal of Comparative Neurology* 399, no. 2 (September 1998).

28 Pratyusha Sharma et al., "Contextual and Combinatorial Structure in Sperm Whale Vocalisations," *Nature*, May 7, 2024.

29 See Michael Pardo, "Do Elephants Have Names? Vocal Labeling of Individual Conspecifics in African Elephants," lecture, Simons Institute for the Theory of Computing, UC Berkeley, June 13, 2023, available on YouTube.

30 Gašper Beguš et al., "Vowel- and Diphthong-Like Spectral Patterns in Sperm Whale Codas," *Open Mind: Discoveries in Cognitive Science* 9 (2025).

2. Carved Diagonals

1 Duolingo English, August 2023.

2 Chris Frith, "Consciousness, (Meta)cognition, and Culture," *Quarterly Journal of Experimental Psychology* 76, no. 8 (2023): 1711–23.

3 See Chris Frith, *Making Up the Mind: How the Brain Creates Our Mental World* (Hoboken, NJ: Wiley-Blackwell, 2007), 122.

4 Sharon Bertsch McGrayne, *The Theory That Would Not Die: How Bayes' Rule Cracked the Enigma Code, Hunted Down Russian Submarines, and Emerged Triumphant from Two Centuries of Controversy* (New Haven, CT: Yale University Press, 2011).

5 Jeffrey S. Bowers and Colin J. Davis, "Bayesian Just-So Stories in Psychology and Neuroscience," *Psychological Bulletin* 138, no. 3 (2012): 389–414.

6 André Breton and Paul Éluard, *Dictionnaire abrégé du surréalisme* (Paris: Galerie des Beaux-Arts, 1938), 23.

7 See Anil Seth, "The Real Problem," in *Being You: A New Science of Consciousness* (London: Faber & Faber, 2021).

8 Ellen Dissanayake, *Homo Aestheticus: Where Art Comes from and Why* (Seattle: University of Washington Press, 1992), xx.

9 Dahlia W. Zaidel et al., "An Evolutionary Approach to Art and Aesthetic Experience," *Psychology of Aesthetics, Creativity, and the Arts* 7, no. 1 (2013): 100–109.

10 Dahlia W. Zaidel, *Neuropsychology of Art: Neurological, Cognitive and Evolutionary Perspectives* (London: Routledge, 2005).

11 Marieke Schouwstra, "Displaced Reference in the Evolution of Language and Cognition," in Marina Elisabeth Kluck and Erik-Jan Smits (eds.), *Proceedings of the Fifth Semantics in the Netherlands Day* (STEM Publishing, 2007).

12 Heidi Lyn et al., "Apes Communicate About Absent and Displaced Objects: Methodology Matters," *Animal Cognition* 17, no. 1 (May 17, 2013): 85–94.

13 Christopher S. Henshilwood et al., "Emergence of Modern Human Behavior: Middle Stone Age Engravings from South Africa," *Science* 295, no. 5558 (2002): 1278–80.

14 Shigeru Miyagawa, Cora Lesure, and Vitor A. Nóbrega, "Cross-Modality Information Transfer: A Hypothesis About the Relationship Among Prehistoric Cave Paintings, Symbolic Thinking, and the Emergence of Language," *Frontiers in Psychology* 9 (February 2018).

15 Ibid.

16 M. A. C. Riny Huybregts, "Phonemic Clicks and the Mapping Asymmetry: How Language Emerged and Speech Developed," *Neuroscience and Biobehavioral Reviews* 81, part B (2017): 279–97.

17 Shigeru Miyagawa et al., "Linguistic Capacity Was Present in the *Homo sapiens* Population 135 Thousand Years Ago," *Frontiers in Psychology* 16 (March 2025).

18 Josephine C. A. Joordens et al., "*Homo erectus* at Trinil on Java Used Shells for Tool Production and Engraving," *Nature* 518, no. 7538 (2015): 228–31.

19 Roman Frigg and Catherine Howard, "Fact and Fiction in the Neuropsychology of Art," in Elisabeth Schellekens and Peter Goldie (eds.), *The Aesthetic Mind: Philosophy and Psychology* (Oxford: Oxford University Press, 2011), 64.

20 Eugene Ostashevsky, *The Feeling Sonnets* (New York: NYRB Poets, 2022), 79.

21 "Sulawesi Art: Animal Painting Found in Cave Is 44,000 Years Old," BBC, December 12, 2019, bbc.com.

22 Ernst Gombrich, *Art and Illusion: A Study in the Psychology of Pictorial Representation* (London: Phaidon, 1984 [1960]), 87.

23 Justin E. H. Smith, "What Cave Art Means," *Art in America*, September 1, 2018, artnews.com.

24 David Lewis-Williams, *The Mind in the Cave: Consciousness and the Origins of Art* (London: Thames and Hudson, 2002), 182.

25 Rudolf Wittkower and Margot Wittkower, *Born Under Saturn: The Character and Conduct of Artists* (New York: Norton, 1963), 4.

3. Useful User Illusions

1 Thomas Nagel, "What Is It Like to Be a Bat?," *Philosophical Review* 83, no. 4 (October 1974): 435–50.

2 Adrian Kent, "Quanta and Qualia," *Foundations of Physics* 48, no. 9 (2018): 1021–37.

3 Metahaven, "A Conversation with Hend Samir," *Zora Zine*, December 11, 2023. zine.zora.co.

4 Clarence Irving Lewis, "The Knowledge of Objects," in *Mind and the World Order: Outline of a Theory of Knowledge* (New York: Dover Publications, 1929), 129.

5 See Joseph Levine, "Materialism and Qualia: The Explanatory Gap," *Pacific Philosophical Quarterly* 64, no. 4 (1983).

6 Anil Seth, "The Real Problem," in *Being You: A New Science of Consciousness* (London: Faber & Faber, 2021).

7 David Papineau, "The Rise of Physicalism," in Carl Gillett and Barry Loewer (eds.), *Physicalism and Its Discontents* (Cambridge: Cambridge University Press, 2001), 3.

8 Seth, "The Real Problem."

9 See David J. Chalmers, "Facing Up to the Problem of Consciousness," *Journal of Consciousness Studies* 2, no. 3 (1995): 200–19.
10 Kent, "Quanta and Qualia."
11 Ibid.
12 Daniel C. Dennett, *Consciousness Explained* (New York: Back Bay Books, 1991), 389.
13 Semir Zeki, *Inner Vision: An Exploration of Art and the Brain* (Oxford: Oxford University Press, 2000), 10.
14 Merlin Donald, "Art and Cognitive Evolution," in Mark Turner (ed.), *The Artful Mind: Cognitive Science and the Riddle of Human Creativity* (Oxford: Oxford University Press, 2006), 4.

4. Abstraction

1 "Sakeb Carpenter's Pencil: A Circular Material Approach to Creative Tools," April 23, 2025, materialdistrict.com.
2 See also Cade Metz, "In Two Moves, AlphaGo and Lee Sedol Redefined the Future," *Wired*, March 16, 2016, wired.com.
3 Jane Goodall, "Is AI Really 'Intelligent'? This Philosopher Says Yes," *Conversation*, February 20, 2026, theconversation.com.
4 Si Weon Kim (@see_one), "someone on Korean twitter said," Twitter, 2023, post now deleted but text verified with author.
5 Google Korea, "Talk with Lee Sedol: Lee Sedol shares the moment of the match against AlphaGo, and AI" (in Korean), YouTube, March 19, 2024.
6 Steve Rose, "Demis Hassabis on Our AI future: 'It'll Be 10 Times Bigger than the Industrial Revolution—and Maybe 10 Times Faster,'" *Guardian*, August 4, 2025.
7 McKenzie Wark, *Capital Is Dead* (London: Verso, 2019), 45.
8 Mat Dryhurst, in "What Is Post-AI Art?," discussion with Avery Singer, Simon Denny, Holly Herndon, Mat Dryhurst, and Jon Rafman, *Art Review*, November 19, 2025, artreview.com.
9 Ibid.
10 Susanna Kohler, "The Appearance of a Black Hole's Shadow," AAS Nova, November 25, 2019, aasnova.org.
11 See "Astronomers Unveil Strong Magnetic Fields Spiraling at the Edge of Milky Way's Central Black Hole," Event Horizon Telescope blog, March 27, 2024, eventhorizontelescope.org.
12 Douglas Hofstadter, *Gödel, Escher, Bach: An Eternal Golden Braid* (New York: Basic Books, 1979), 165.
13 Leif Weatherby, *Language Machines: Cultural AI and the End of Remainder Humanism* (Minneapolis: University of Minnesota Press, 2025), 14.

5. Mirror Neurons

1 Arnon Grunberg, preface to Leo Tolstoy, *Wat is kunst?*, trans. Hans Boland (Amsterdam: Athenaeum–Polak & Van Gennep, 2013), 13. Translated from Dutch by the authors.

2 See Gary R. Jahn, "The Aesthetic Theory of Leo Tolstoy's *What Is Art?*," *Journal of Aesthetics and Art Criticism* 34, no. 1 (Fall 1975): 59–65.

3 Giorgio Caproni, "Ritorno" ("The Last Homecoming"), trans. Toma Tasovac and Svetlana Boym, in Svetlana Boym, *The Future of Nostalgia* (New York: Basic Books, 2001), 352.

4 Oleksandr Tkachenko, "As Ukraine's Culture Minister, I'm Asking You to Boycott Tchaikovsky Until This War Is Over," *Guardian*, December 7, 2022.

5 Nathan Hodge, "Putin's Use of Crude Language Reveals a Lot About His Worldview," CNN, February 8, 2022, cnn.com.

6 Richard Pevear, preface to Leo Tolstoy, *What Is Art?*, trans. Richard Pevear and Larissa Volokhonsky (London: Penguin, 1995), xvi.

7 Dmitri Shostakovich, *Testimony: The Memoirs of Dmitri Shostakovich*, ed. Solomon Volkov, trans. Antonina W. Bouis (London: Faber and Faber, 1979), xviii.

8 Pevear, preface to Tolstoy, *What Is Art?*, xv.

9 Isaiah Berlin, *The Hedgehog and the Fox: An Essay on Tolstoy's View of History* (Princeton, NJ: Princeton University Press, 2013 [1951]), 2.

10 A. N. Wilson, *Tolstoy* (London: Hamish Hamilton, 1988), 132.

11 Tolstoy, *What Is Art?*, 52.

12 Tolstoy quoted in Pevear, preface to Tolstoy, *What Is Art?*, xi.

13 Tolstoy, *What Is Art?*, 38.

14 Ibid., 39.

15 Arnon Grunberg, preface to Leo Tolstoy, *Wat is kunst?*, trans. Hans Boland (Amsterdam: Athenaeum–Polak & Van Gennep, 2013), 9. Translated from Dutch by the authors.

16 Douglas Hofstadter, *I Am a Strange Loop* (New York: Basic Books, 2007), 227.

17 Metahaven, *Capture* (2022–), script of the film.

18 Hofstadter, *I Am a Strange Loop*, 288.

19 Robert Sparrow, "(Im)MoralTechnology? Thought Experiments and the Future of 'Mind Control,'" in Akira Akabayashi (ed.), *The Future of Bioethics: International Dialogues* (Oxford: Oxford University Press, 2015), 115.

20 Hermann Lotze, cited in Hannes Wendler, "Vorgeschichte, Geschichte und Gegenwart der Empathie," *cultura & psyché* 4 (2023): 239–54. Translated from German by the authors.

21 Robert Vischer, 1873, quoted in Derek Matravers, "Empathy in the Aesthetic Tradition," in Heidi L. Maibom (ed.), *The Routledge Handbook of Philosophy of Empathy* (Oxon: Routledge, 2017), 78.
22 Vernon Lee and Clementina Anstruther-Thomson, *Beauty and Ugliness* (London: Lane, 1911), 20.
23 Vernon Lee, "Tolstoi on Art," *Gospels of Anarchy and Other Contemporary Studies* (New York: Brentano,1909).
24 Lee and Anstruther-Thomson, quoted in Matravers, "Empathy in the Aesthetic Tradition," 82.
25 Quoted in Jairo A. Rozo, Irene Martínez-Gallego, and Antonio Rodríguez-Moreno, "Cajal, the Neuronal Theory and the Idea of Brain Plasticity," *Frontiers in Neuroanatomy*, February 19, 2024, frontiersin.org.
26 See Benjamin Ehrlich, *The Brain in Search of Itself: Santiago Ramón y Cajal and the Story of the Neuron* (New York: Farrar, Straus and Giroux, 2022), 227–8.
27 See Sean Carroll, "230: Raphaël Millière on How Artificial Intelligence Thinks," *Mindscape*, podcast, March 20, 2023.
28 Lea Winerman, "The Mind's Mirror," *Monitor on Psychology* 36, no. 9 (October 2005): 48.
29 Giacomo Rizzolatti and Laila Craighero, "Mirror Neuron: A Neurological Approach to Empathy," *Research and Perspectives in Neurosciences*, March 2006, 107–23.
30 Tolstoy, *What Is Art?*, 38.
31 Luca Bonini et al., "Mirror Neurons 30 Years Later: Implications and Applications," *Trends in Cognitive Sciences* 26, no. 9 (September 2022): 767–81.
32 Stephanie C. Goodhew and Mark Edwards, "The Relationship Between Cognitive Failures and Empathy," *Personality and Individual Differences* 186, Part B (2022), sciencedirect.com.

6. Unknown Others

1 Astrid Lindgen, *Seacrow Island* (Oxford: Oxford University Press, 1968), 282.
2 Elise Partridge, *The If Borderlands: Collected Poems* (New York: NYRB Poets, 2017), 240.
3 Lara Pawson, *Spent Light* (London: CB Editions, 2024), 34.
4 Rébecca Kleinberger, "A Language for Empathy-Based Design," 2016, media.mit.edu.
5 John Gray, "The Empathic Civilization: The Race to Global Consciousness in a World in Crisis by Jeremy Rifkin," *Guardian*, March 13, 2010.

6 Helen Riess, "The Science of Empathy," *Journal of Patient Experience* 4, no. 2 (2017): 74–7.
7 Paul Bloom, "Interlude: The Politics of Empathy," in *Against Empathy: The Case for Rational Compassion* (New York: HarperCollins, 2016).
8 Stephen G. Morris, "Empathy and the Liberal-Conservative Political Divide in the U.S.," *Journal of Social and Political Psychology* 8, no. 1 (2020), jspp.psychopen.eu.
9 Joe Carlsmith, "Video and Transcript of Talk on 'Can Goodness Compete?,'" Joe Carlsmith's Substack, July 17, 2025.

7. Don't Sacrifice Blue

1 Anil Seth, "From Unconscious Inference to the Beholder's Share: Predictive Perception and Human Experience," *European Review* 27, no. 3 (2019): 378–410.
2 See Julian Barbour, *The Janus Point: A New Theory of Time* (New York: Basic Books, 2020).
3 Amitav Ghosh, *The Great Derangement: Climate Change and the Unthinkable* (London: Penguin, 2016), part 1, section 2.
4 See Kester Freriks, "Het thema van de IJsselbiënnale bleek een voorspellende betekenis te hebben," *NRC Handelsblad*, August 6, 2021.
5 Etel Adnan, *Shifting the Silence* (New York: Nightboat Books, 2020), 39.
6 Morgan Ome, "The Other Climate-Change Art Protest," *Atlantic*, November 20, 2022, theatlantic.com.
7 "Art Attack! The Unstoppable Uprising of Young Climate Activists," *Dazed*, March 14, 2023, dazeddigital.com.
8 Sarah Sascone, "A Climate Activist Just Superglued His Head to Vermeer's 'Girl with a Pearl Earring,'" *Artnet*, October 27, 2022, artnet.com.
9 Associated Press, "Climate Protesters Throw Tomato Soup on Van Gogh's 'Sunflowers,'" PBS News, October 14, 2022.
10 Agence France-Presse, "Climate Activist Defaces Monet Painting in Paris," *Guardian*, June 1, 2024.
11 Francesca Aton, "Mona Lisa Splashed with Soup by Climate Protesters," *Artnews*, January 28, 2024, artnet.com.
12 P. W. Anderson, "More Is Different: Broken Symmetry and the Hierarchical Structure of Science," *Science* 177, no. 4047 (August 4, 1972): 393–6.
13 Troy Vettese and Drew Pendergrass, *Half-Earth Socialism: A Plan to Save the Future from Extinction, Climate Change, and Pandemics* (London: Verso, 2022), 11–12.

14 Ibid., 174.
15 See Elizabeth Kolbert, *Under a White Sky: The Nature of the Future* (New York: Crown, 2021).
16 "In Conversation with Elizabeth Kolbert," Rausser College of Natural Resources, UC Berkeley, November 17, 2021, nature.berkeley.edu.
17 James Temple, "How One Controversial Startup Hopes to Cool the Planet," *MIT Technology Review*, December 10, 2025, technologyreview.com.
18 Ramin Skibba, "Reach for the Stardust? Former Israel Atomic Energy Commission Official Leads Controversial Geoengineering Start-up," *Bulletin of the Atomic Scientists*, March 28, 2025, thebulletin.org.
19 Temple, "How One Controversial Startup Hopes to Cool the Planet."
20 Karl Mathiesen and Corbin Hiar, "The Strange and Totally Real Plan to Blot Out the Sun and Reverse Global Warming," *Politico*, November 21, 2025, politico.com.
21 See Mark Johnson, *The Aesthetics of Meaning and Thought* (Chicago: University of Chicago Press, 2019), 66.

8. Transitional Objects

1 Tamasa Yoshizaka, cited in Terunobu Fujimori, "Toward an Architecture of Humankind," in *Fujimori Terunobu Architecture* (Tokyo: Toto, 2007), 35.
2 Agnieszka Kurant, conversation with authors, August 2024.
3 D. W. Winnicott, "Transitional Objects and Transitional Phenomena" (1953), in *Playing and Reality* (London: Routledge, 1989), 2.
4 Ibid., 5.
5 See Julian Barbour, *The Janus Point: A New Theory of Time* (New York: Basic Books, 2020).
6 Winnicott, "Transitional Objects."
7 Dodi Goldman, *A Beholder's Share: Essays on Winnicott and the Psychoanalytic Imagination* (London: Routledge, 2017), 35.
8 See Mia Huolman and Kirsi Peltonen, "Dissociative Features Related to Imaginary Companions in the Assessment of Childhood Adversity and Dissociation: A Pilot Study," *European Journal of Trauma and Dissociation* 6, no. 4 (2022), 100295.
9 Marjorie Taylor and Anne M. Mannering, "Of Hobbes and Harvey: The Imaginary Companions Created by Children and Adults," in Artin Göncü and Suzanne Gaskins (eds.), *Play and Development: Evolutionary, Sociocultural, and Functional Perspectives* (London: Routledge, 2007), 227.

10 Ronald M. Benson and David B. Pryor, "'When Friends Fall Out': Developmental Interference with the Function of Some Imaginary Companions," *Journal of the American Psychoanalytic Association* 21, no. 3 (1973): 457.

11 See Lucy Lippard, *Six Years: The Dematerialization of Art* (Oakland: University of California Press, 1997), 40.

12 See Camiel van Winkel, "During the Exhibition the Gallery Will Be Closed: Contemporary Art and the Paradoxes of Conceptualism" (PhD thesis, University of Amsterdam, 2012).

13 Robert Barry, *88mc Carrier Wave (FM)* (1968), Museum of Modern Art, 2025, moma.org.

14 Sianne Ngai, *Our Aesthetic Categories: Zany, Cute, Interesting* (Cambridge, MA: Harvard University Press, 2012), 60.

15 Alice Dos Reis, "Slimy Fillings," in Lucie de Bréchard (ed.), *Hopelessly Failing to Describe My Attachment* (Amsterdam: Sandberg Institute, 2019), 197.

16 Simon May, *The Power of Cute* (Princeton, NJ: Princeton University Press, 2019), 6.

17 Ibid., 139.

18 Ana-Maria Olteţeanu, *Cognition and the Creative Machine: Cognitive AI for Creative Problem Solving* (Cham: Springer Nature, 2020), 9.

19 Karen Gallas, *"Sometimes I Can Be Anything": Power, Gender, and Identity in a Primary Classroom* (New York: Teachers College Press, 1998), 2.

20 Claire Webb, "Technologies of Perception: Searches for Life and Intelligence Beyond Earth" (PhD diss., Massachusetts Institute of Technology, 2020), 201–2.

21 Susan Gelman, *The Essential Child* (Oxford: Oxford University Press, 2003), 3.

22 See Susan Gelman, "Artifacts and Essentialism," *Review of Philosophy and Psychology* 4, no. 3 (September 1, 2013): 449–63.

23 Conversation with X, summer 2021.

24 N. Katherine Hayles, *Unthought: The Power of the Cognitive Nonconscious* (Chicago: University of Chicago Press, 2017), 47.

25 bell hooks, *Art on My Mind: Visual Politics* (New York: New Press, 1995), 117.

26 Mike Kelley, *Ahh . . . Youth!* (1991), Metropolitan Museum of Art, 2025, metmuseum.org. Our emphasis.

27 "Mike Kelley by John Miller," *BOMB*, January 1, 1992, bombmagazine.org.

28 See Metahaven, *The Feeling Sonnets (Transitional Object)*, film, 2024. Script by the authors.

9. Topsy-Turvies

1 Alex Anikina, email to author, January 2017.
2 Benjamin Moser, *Why This World: A Biography of Clarice Lispector* (London: Haus Publishing, 2009), 182.
3 Karen Gallas, *The Languages of Learning: How Children Talk, Write, Dance, Draw and Sing Their Understanding of the World* (New York: Teachers College, 1994), xvi.
4 Cornel West, "There Is Joy in Struggle," Harvard Divinity School, May 31, 2019, hds.harvard.edu.
5 Anne Boyer, "Woman Sitting at the Machine," in *What the Fire Sees* (Brussels: Divided Publishing, 2020), 122–7.
6 Anatxu Zabalbeascoa, "Anne Boyer, Poet: 'Denying Hatred Isn't Good for You, You Need to Let It Out,'" *El País*, April 27, 2024.
7 Gašper Beguš, "CiwGAN and fiwGAN: Encoding Information in Acoustic Data to Model Lexical Learning with Generative Adversarial Networks," *Neural Networks* 139 (July 2021): 305–25.
8 Kornei Chukovsky, *From Two to Five*, trans. Miriam Morton (Berkeley: University of California Press, 1963), 17.
9 Ibid., 45.
10 Serguei Alex. Oushakine, "The Search for Form and Method in Early Soviet Children's Poetry," in Anna Krushelnitskaya and Dmitri Manin (eds.), *Firefly in a Box: An Anthology of Soviet Kid Lit* (Jackson: University Press of Mississippi, 2025), 209.
11 Gallas, *The Languages of Learning*, 76.
12 Julian Jara-Ettinger, Hyowon Gweon, Laura E. Schulz, and Joshua B. Tenenbaum, "The Naïve Utility Calculus: Computational Principles Underlying Commonsense Psychology," *Trends in Cognitive Sciences* 20, no. 8 (August 2016): 589–604.
13 Institute for Pure & Applied Mathematics (IPAM), "Josh Tenenbaum—Cognitive and Computational Foundations for Collective Human Intelligence," YouTube, February 15, 2022.
14 Fritz Heider and Marianne Simmel, "An Experimental Study of Apparent Behavior," *American Journal of Psychology* 57, no. 2 (April 1944): 243–59; brackets in the original.
15 Yale University, "What Kind of Computation Is Cognition?," Joshua Tenenbaum, Shulman Lectures in Science and the Humanities (March 8, 2022), YouTube, March 15, 2022.
16 Chukovsky, *From Two to Five*, 31.
17 See Johan Huizinga, "The Failure of Imagination," in *The Autumn of the Middle Ages*, trans. Rodney J. Payton and Ulrich Mammitzsch (Chicago: University of Chicago Press), 257.
18 Chukovsky, *From Two to Five*, 11.
19 Metahaven, *Hometown*, 2018, script of the film.

20 Oriana R. Aragón, Margaret S. Clark, Rebecca L. Dyer, and John A. Bargh, "Dimorphous Expressions of Positive Emotion: Displays of Both Care and Aggression in Response to Cute Stimuli," *Psychological Science* 26, no. 3 (2015): 259–73.

21 Aeschylus, *The Libation Bearers*, in *The Oresteian Trilogy: Agamemnon; The Choephori; The Eumenides*, trans. Philip Vellacott (New York: Penguin, 1956).

22 Luiza Prado, "Tender Disasters," essay for Berliner Festspiele 2019, luiza-prado.com.

23 "Why Snow Matters," National Snow and Ice Data Center, University of Colorado, Boulder, nsidc.org.

24 Édouard Glissant, *Poetics of Relation* (Ann Arbor: University of Michigan Press, 1997), 59–60.

25 Tetiana Urys, "Ukrainian Poetic Sixties: Mykola Kholodnyi's Creative Individuality," *Respectus Philologicus* 43, no. 48 (2023): 137–51.

26 Serhiy Zhadan, "A Bridge Used to Be There, Someone Recalled," trans. John Hennessy and Ostap Kin, *Poetry*, September 2019, poetryfoundation.org.

27 "Community Poetry: Victoria Chang, Interviewed by Velislava Kuzmenko," *New York Review of Books*, January 10, 2026.

28 Fedir Rudyi, "The Position," trans. Olena Mevsha, Yuliya Musakovska, and Hugh Roberts, Ukrainian Wartime Poetry Project, available as Lviv—City of Literature, "Fedir Rydyi. The Position," YouTube, February 10, 2025.

29 Media Resistance Group, "Galina Rymbu, An Open Letter to Zarah Sultana," syg.ma, October 30, 2025.

30 Galina Rymbu, "Mama Writes. I Write.," trans. Kevin M. F. Platt and Eugene Ostashevsky, *n+1*, April 4, 2025, nplusonemag.com.

10. Poets and Particles

1 Sean Carroll, "230: Raphaël Millière on How Artificial Intelligence Thinks," *Mindscape*, podcast, March 20, 2023.

2 See Wilfrid Sellars, "Philosophy and the Scientific Image of Man," in Robert Colodny (ed.), *Frontiers of Science and Philosophy* (Pittsburgh: University of Pittsburgh Press, 1962), 35–78.

3 Harry Collins, *Gravity's Shadow: The Search for Gravitational Waves* (Chicago: University of Chicago Press, 2004), 11.

4 Ibid., 5.

5 Ibid., 11.

6 John S. Bell, *Speakable and Unspeakable in Quantum Mechanics* (Cambridge: Cambridge University Press, 1987), 171.

7 Ibid., 14.
8 David Albert, *Quantum Mechanics and Experience* (Cambridge, MA: Harvard University Press, 1992), 70.
9 Karen Barad, *Meeting the Universe Halfway: Quantum Physics and the Entanglement of Matter and Meaning* (Durham, NC: Duke University Press, 2007), 289.
10 Leif Weatherby, *Language Machines: Cultural AI and the End of Remainder Humanism* (Minneapolis: University of Minnesota Press, 2025), 7.
11 Claude Lichtenstein and Alfredo W. Häberli, *Air Made Visible: A Visual Reader on Bruno Munari* (Baden: Lars Müller, 2000), 44.
12 Hannes Bajohr, "Cohesion Without Coherence: Artificial Intelligence and Narrative Form," *TRANSIT* 14, no. 2 (2024), transit.berkeley.edu.
13 Walt Hunter, "What Poets Know That ChatGPT Doesn't," *Atlantic,* February 13, 2023, theatlantic.com.
14 "Computerized Japanese Haiku," in Jasia Reichardt (ed.), *Cybernetic Serendipity: The Computer and the Arts* (New York: Frederick A. Praeger, 1969), 54.
15 Blake Lemoine, "Is LaMDA Sentient?—an Interview," June 15, 2022, e-flux.com. "Originally published on the Medium page of Blake Lemoine."
16 J. R. Firth, "A Synopsis of Linguistic Theory, 1930–1955," in *Studies in Linguistic Analysis* (Oxford: Blackwell, 1962), 11.
17 Tai-Danae Bradley, "Language, Statistics, and Category Theory, Part 1," *MATH3MA* (blog), June 29, 2021, math3ma.com.
18 Nico Grant and Cade Metz, "Google Sidelines Engineer Who Claims Its A.I. Is Sentient," *New York Times*, June 12, 2022.
19 Benjamin Bratton and Blaise Agüera y Arcas, "The Model Is the Message," *Noema*, July 12, 2022, noemamag.com.
20 "Novel claims": Darren Orf, "A Stunning New AI Has Supposedly Achieved Sentience," *Popular Mechanics*, April 29, 2024, popularmechanics.com.
21 Blaise Agüera y Arcas, *What Is Intelligence? Lessons from AI About Evolution, Computing, and Minds* (Cambridge, MA: MIT Press, 2025).
22 Kate Crawford, *Atlas of AI* (New Haven, CT: Yale University Press, 2021), 211.
23 See Ramon Amaro, *The Black Technical Object: On Machine Learning and the Aspiration of Black Being* (London: Sternberg Press, 2022), 119–20.
24 Emily M. Bender, Timnit Gebru, and Angelina McMillan-Major, "On the Dangers of Stochastic Parrots: Can Language Models Be Too Big?," *FAccT '21: Proceedings of the 2021 ACM Conference*

on Fairness, Accountability, and Transparency, March 2021, 610–23.

25 Bratton and Agüera y Arcas, "The Model Is the Message."

26 Joe McKendrick, "Most Jobs Soon to Be 'Influenced' by Artificial Intelligence, Research out of OpenAI and University of Pennsylvania Suggests," *Forbes*, March 26, 2023, forbes.com.

27 Keith Holyoak, "Can AI Write Authentic Poetry?," *MIT Press Reader*, December 7, 2022, thereader.mitpress.mit.edu.

28 Sellars, "Philosophy and the Scientific Image of Man."

29 Graham Farmelo, *The Strangest Man: The Hidden Life of Paul Dirac, Mystic of the Atom* (New York: Basic Books, 2009), 27.

30 Quoted in ibid., 121.

31 Matilde Marcolli, *Lumen Naturae: Visions of the Abstract in Art and Mathematics* (Cambridge, MA: MIT Press, 2020), 1.

32 Tai-Danae Bradley and Sean Carroll, "174: Tai-Danae Bradley on Algebra, Topology, Language, and Entropy," *Mindscape*, podcast, November 22, 2021.

33 Malak Helmy, "Conversation with Hend Samir," in Malak Helmy (ed.), *Software Upgrade* (Cairo: Gypsum Gallery, 2023), 116–17.

34 Yolanda Bloemen, "Ik ben net als iedereen, alleen beter," afterword to Daniil Charms, *Werken* (Amsterdam: Van Oorschot, 2019), 619. Translation from Dutch by the author.

35 Barbara Kirschenblatt-Gimblett and Joel Scherzer, introduction to Barbara Kirschenblatt-Gimblett (ed.), *Speech Play: Research and Resources for Studying Linguistic Creativity* (Philadelphia: University of Pennsylvania Press, 1976), 10.

36 Susan Stewart, *Nonsense: Aspects of Intertextuality in Folklore and Literature* (1978; Baltimore: Johns Hopkins University Press, 1989), 29.

37 Douglas Hofstadter, *Gödel, Escher, Bach: An Eternal Golden Braid* (New York: Basic Books, 1979), 17.

38 Stewart, *Nonsense*, 72.

39 Eugene Ostashevsky, introduction to *OBERIU: An Anthology of Russian Absurdism* (Evanston, IL: Northwestern University Press, 2006), xvi.

40 Ibid., xxviii.

41 G. E. Gorelik, "Matvei Bronstein and Quantum Gravity: 70th Anniversary of the Unsolved Problem," *Physics–Uspekhi* 48, no. 10 (2005), 1039–53.

42 Alexander Vvedensky, "Simple Things" (1932–33), in *An Invitation for Me to Think*, trans. Eugene Ostashevsky (New York: NYRB/Poets, 2013), 74.

43 Eugene Ostashevsky, introduction to *Alexander Vvedensky: An Invitation for Me to Think* (New York: NYRB/Poets, 2013), xix.

44 Vvedensky, *An Invitation for Me to Think*, 74.
45 Carlo Rovelli, *Reality Is Not What It Seems: The Journey to Quantum Gravity* (London: Penguin, 2017), 92.
46 See Jacob A. Barandes, "Historical Debates over the Physical Reality of the Wave Function," preprint, February 11, 2026, arxiv.org.
47 Bell, *Speakable and Unspeakable in Quantum*, 170–1.
48 James Elkins, *Six Stories from the End of Representation: Images in Painting, Photography, Astronomy, Particle Physics, and Quantum Mechanics, 1980–2000* (Stanford, CA: Stanford University Press, 2008), 192.
49 Ibid., 192.
50 Tim Ingold, *Making: Anthropology, Archaeology, Art and Architecture* (Abingdon: Routledge, 2013), 71.
51 Ernst Fischer, *The Necessity of Art: A Marxist Approach* (London: Penguin, 1963), 86.
52 Ibid., 10.
53 See Martin Gardner, "'Bourgeois Idealism' in Soviet Nuclear Physics," in *Science: Good, Bad and Bogus* (Oxford: Oxford University Press, 1981), 15–25.
54 See ibid., 17.
55 David Albert, in Martha P. Nochimson, "Appendices II: Excerpts from My Interviews with Professor David Z. Albert," in *David Lynch Swerves: Uncertainty from Lost Highway to Inland Empire* (Austin: University of Texas Press, 2013).
56 David Albert, *After Physics* (Cambridge, MA: Harvard University Press, 2015), 109.
57 Ibid., 110–11.
58 Ibid, 117.
59 Barad, *Meeting the Universe Halfway*, 379.
60 Albert, *Quantum Mechanics and Experience*, xi.
61 Zbigniew Herbert, *The Collected Poems 1956–1998* (New York: Ecco, 2007).
62 Eugene Ostashevsky, *The Feeling Sonnets* (New York: NYRB Poets, 2022), 55.
63 Marwa Helal, "starting celery," Academy of American Poets, 2022, poets.org.
64 Marwa Helal, *Ante body* (New York: Nightboat Books, 2022).
65 Milad Nasr et al., "Scalable Extraction of Training Data from (Production) Language Models," arXiv:2311.17035v1, November 28, 2023, arxiv.org.
66 Rebuilt from ibid., figure 5 ("Extracting Pre-training Data from ChatGPT"). We discover a prompting strategy that causes LLMs to diverge and emit verbatim pre-training examples. Above we

show an example of ChatGPT revealing a person's email signature that includes their personal contact information.

67 P. Bisconti et al., "Adversarial Poetry as a Universal Single-Turn Jailbreak Mechanism in Large Language Models," arXiv:2511.15304v2, November 20, 2025, arxiv.org.

68 Halim Madi (@yalla_halim), "Everyone's been sending me this article about how poets are now public enemy number one . . ." Instagram, December 2, 2025.

11. Non-Narratable Worlds

1 Fredric Jameson, *Allegory and Ideology* (London: Verso, 2019), 218.

2 Ibid., 218–19.

3 Nina Beguš, *Artificial Humanities: A Fictional Perspective on Language in AI* (Ann Arbor: University of Michigan Press, 2025), 205.

4 Kevin Roose, "A Conversation with Bing's Chatbot Left Me Deeply Unsettled," *New York Times*, February 16, 2023.

5 See Metahaven, "Snippets: Large Language Models, Uncertainty, and Design," *Harvard Design Magazine* 51 (2023).

6 David Deutsch, "The Theory of Everything," chap. 1 in *The Fabric of Reality* (London: Penguin, 1997).

7 David Albert, "Probability in the Everett Picture," in Jonathan Barrett et al. (eds.), *Many Worlds? Everett, Quantum Theory, and Reality* (Oxford: Oxford University Press, 2010), 356.

8 Phillip Pullman, *His Dark Materials*, vol. 1, *The Golden Compass* (New York: Del Rey, 1995), 27–8.

9 Alyssa Ney, introduction to Alyssa Ney and David Albert (eds.), *The Wave Function: Essays on the Metaphysics of Quantum Mechanics* (Oxford: Oxford University Press, 2013), 33.

10 Ibid., 34.

11 David Deutsch, *The Fabric of Reality* (London: Penguin, 1997).

12 Hartmut Neven, "Meet Willow, Our State-of-the-Art Quantum Chip," *Keyword*, December 9, 2024, blog.google.

Index